T0354824

Nurture II A Nurturing Approach to Trauma

Nurture II A Nurturing Approach to Trauma

What Happened to Mariah?

Dr. Mattie Lee Jones

NURTURE II A NURTURING APPROACH TO TRAUMA
WHAT HAPPENED TO MARIAH?

Copyright © 2024 Dr. Mattie Lee Jones.

All rights reserved. No part of this book may be used or reproduced by any means, graphic, electronic, or mechanical, including photocopying, recording, taping or by any information storage retrieval system without the written permission of the author except in the case of brief quotations embodied in critical articles and reviews.

iUniverse books may be ordered through booksellers or by contacting:

iUniverse
1663 Liberty Drive
Bloomington, IN 47403
www.iuniverse.com
844-349-9409

Because of the dynamic nature of the Internet, any web addresses or links contained in this book may have changed since publication and may no longer be valid. The views expressed in this work are solely those of the author and do not necessarily reflect the views of the publisher, and the publisher hereby disclaims any responsibility for them.

Any people depicted in stock imagery provided by Getty Images are models, and such images are being used for illustrative purposes only.
Certain stock imagery © Getty Images.

ISBN: 978-1-6632-6443-5 (sc)
ISBN: 978-1-6632-6444-2 (e)

Print information available on the last page.

iUniverse rev. date: 07/15/2024

What Happened to Mariah?

What conclusion do you come to about a person who may have alcohol use disorder, a drug addiction, homelessness, living on the street, or isolated, and afraid to trust anyone? I desire that after you read Nurture II, your thoughts lead you to consider asking the question, "What happened to them?" and that you may also be determined to be a nurturing addition to the lives of the children you interact with.

This book is dedicated to those making it possible for children to grow into adulthood as healthy as possible by surrounding them with love and nurture.

With God All Things are Possible

Matthew 19:26

Contents

Contents

PART ONE

Introduction

The first edition of Nurture, published in 2016, revealed the importance of developing and connecting children's social, emotional, and cognitive development by creating nurturing environments and experiences. The book also discussed the importance of research and expertise to ensure that all early learners obtain nurturing experiences from those who care for and teach them.

The second edition of Nurture is an extension that includes a close look at the effects of trauma on children's ability to learn and thrive and how a nurturing approach to trauma combats its lasting effects on children's growing brains.

From the start, you will obtain a broad understanding of what trauma is and a psychological view of how a young brain responds. A clear and precise meaning of what a nurturing experience looks like for children and why it is necessary is shared. Understanding that nurture is not just a term but an action. I view nurture as an action because it should be a part of our relationships and interactions with all children and others.

Nurture is an important, sometimes overlooked, key to helping children survive traumatic events. This edition will go in-depth about how nurturing relationships foster well-being in children and may change their lives by altering the effects of trauma. I will also briefly share what I have learned from the many years of research that experts have conducted on studying the brain and psychology related to trauma and the importance of nurture.

The original Nurture book is added for review as part two of this edition. This edition will provide a clearer understanding of what it means to be the nurturing person discussed in part two, what it looks like and feels like, and how to relate in a nurturing way that is consistent and intentional.

The first edition of Nurture covered the how, and this edition covers the why and answers the following: What do the terms traumatic events and nurturing experiences mean? What should you expect to hear and see in a nurturing environment? Why is it essential for all children to be in a nurturing environment?

Additionally, the second edition will serve as a way for those with relationships with children to relate to and benefit from the knowledge that being a nurturing person in a child's life will help alleviate some of the pain and damage caused by trauma. A child may be in a traumatic environment at home or have had or is having a traumatic experience that their school, community, and others in their family may not be aware of.

Studies show that children surrounded by nurturing people in nurturing environments develop the social and emotional skills to become resilient and mentally stronger adults than those who do not.

This critical insight is not shared through a research project but through a narrative about a fictional young lady who grew up in the shadow of a traumatic childhood that molded and shaped her adult life. As her life is inscribed throughout her childhood, school years, and into womanhood, I want the reader to understand better why some people may act the way they do. An empathic view of a person who may seem odd, disruptive, or self-destructive may not be unreasonable when taking into consideration the knowledge of the way that those who struggled to survive tragic events as a child with no nurturing relationships to support them may act.

In this edition of Nurture, the depth of how traumatic events can be a leading force in a person's life from childhood to adulthood is played out in the life journey story of Mariah. Mariah is a fictional person; however, the impact of the trauma she endured on who she became is based on my findings from brain science and the social and emotional development of young children.

I hope that Mariah's story will provide insight into trauma in a way that gives reality to the need for personal knowledge and understanding of the power that "Nurture" has in the lives of children.

Dear Reader, before I tell you about Mariah, I want to answer two commonly asked questions: What is trauma? What is meant by nurture?

Many experiences are considered and labeled as traumatic. These experiences or events may be emotional and physical. Studies show that there are levels of both. For this book, I will use the description of trauma as the result of exposure to experiences or events that are emotionally disturbing or disruptive with an overwhelming, lasting, and sometimes irreversible effect on the social-emotional well-being of a child. Mariah's story is an emotionally traumatic journey.

I incorporate nurture as an action. It is the decisive act of promoting a child's healthy development with love, protection, support, and encouragement. After you travel through Mariah's life journey, there will be a summary of the trauma she encountered and the impact that being unnurtured throughout these events had on who she became as a woman.

I want to encourage you to please continue to read or review part two of Nurture II. This book shares the writing of the first edition of Nurture and connects children's social, emotional, and cognitive needs with a nurturing approach.

What Happened to Mariah?

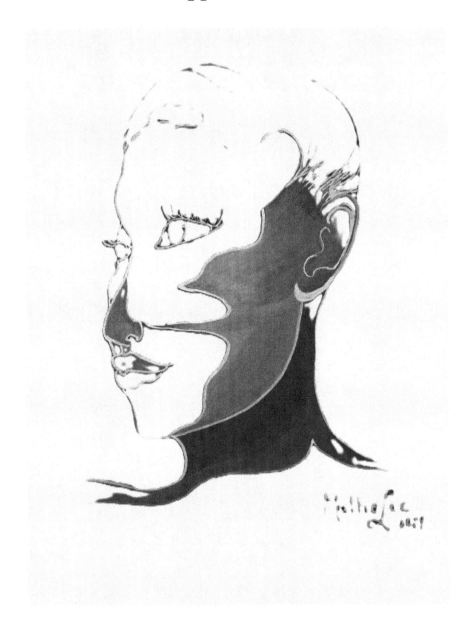

What Happened to Mariah?

As I tell Mariah's story, you may think she is like someone you know, or it may even sound like your story. Although, unfortunately, her childhood experience may be a reality for many men and women, hers is not my story nor anyone I know or have met. I desire that Mariah's life journey will serve as a testament to the importance of nurturing relationships in a child's life.

When Mariah was five, her father left her and her mother. She spent many nights crying and being awakened by the sound of her mother crying. One day, when her mother picked her up from school, she asked if she could visit her father. The mother told her that her father left them for another family and did not want anything to do with either of them. She looked Mariah in the eyes and told her it was her fault that he had left. She then screamed at her and told her never to ask again. Mariah was too young to understand and wondered why her mother did not talk to her after he left.

Her mother worked from home and spent most of her time in her office or bedroom. Even before her father departed from their lives, Mariah did not get to spend time with her mother. Mariah had learned to feed herself by making sandwiches or using the microwave, as her mother kept a supply of frozen dinners.

Mariah's mother had a hard time dealing with and accepting the loss and rejection of her father and treated her bitterly. The bitterness came in belittling remarks and no communication or acknowledgment of Mariah's presence in the house or a room. Four years later, Mariah came home to a house full of strangers and was told that her father had died.

She was introduced to a woman who called herself her grandmother. She had never met this woman, but she found out later that she was her father's mother. Some others there that day said they were family, but she did not know them.

It seemed to Mariah that these people were not just saddened by her father's death but also very angry and not very friendly toward her mother. She heard them talking about her father committing suicide. This left Mariah in a state of shock and confusion. Her mother would not allow her to go to her father's funeral or talk about what happened to him.

When Mirah was in high school, she felt her mother had driven others on both sides of the family out of their lives. One weekend, she tried to get in contact with her mother's sister. Mariah eventually found the phone number and called her aunt. Her Aunt told her she did not think it was a good idea for them to talk. This conversation made her realize she may never have anyone to talk to or trust.

Mariah went into isolating herself and dealt with the rejection of her mother and others by reading books. She did not have or want any friends and went from school to home each day.

Mariah was brilliant and sometimes called an overachiever by her peers. She put all her effort into her schoolwork and received a scholarship to attend college without trying. In her last year of high school, she came home to find that her mother had been admitted to the hospital. The doctor told her that her mother had suffered a nervous breakdown and could not see anyone.

Mariah made it to college and lived on campus. She did not trust anyone and guarded herself by not allowing herself to seek help or need anyone. In college, Mariah was depressed and began to drink alone. Her drinking became a habit because she felt it made her feel better and helped her not to think about what she went through. At this point, she still did not know why she felt so much pain; she only knew that she had felt abandoned and alone all her life. She started to go out to bars around the college campus at night.

After over a year of drinking daily and visiting the bar, she falls into socializing with men at the bar. By her second year in college, she was on academic probation; in year three, she was pregnant and had to leave the college campus dorm.

Mariah leaves college and finds herself deeper into adulthood and alone. She has suffered from fatigue and headaches since high school and is having trouble with the

pregnancy. Disappointed in herself and still unprepared to deal with life as a woman, she finds herself overwhelmed. She is a woman who is now going to be responsible for the life of another human being.

Take a moment to reflect:

What do you think other people who do not know what Mariah went through and is going through believe and say about her behavior?

In the story you read about Mariah, you are briefly taken on the life journey of a fictional character; her unconscious reactions to traumatic events and her lack of nurturing relationships from childhood to adulthood are shared to help provide a clearer understanding of the knowledge exposed from science, psychological studies, and findings and help explain what happened to make Mariah react to life the way she did.

A Deeper Look into What Happened to Mariah

Research shows us that what happened to Mirah results from what can happen to a person not nurtured during childhood. Some traumatic events and experiences, which are also called adverse childhood experiences, will have an impact on the way a child grows up to view themselves and the world.

As a child, Mariah was under-nurtured and had no natural affection from her parents. Her story demonstrates some of the unconscious negative behaviors that can develop and be taken into adulthood as a result of emotional trauma. The emotional abuse she received from her mother and a lack of nurturing after the tragic death of her father influenced her growing brain in a way that was out of her control.

We read in her story that she does not trust anyone and lives a life of isolation before and after high school. As she entered college, she developed destructive relationships and activities.

Studies show that children who grow up neglected and abused carry the effect of this stress on their brains for many years. There are ongoing studies on the impact of trauma on the brain development of young children. One study determined that a critical time for brain development is ages 0-3. This is the time when a child's experiences shape lifelong health. What they experience impacts how they learn and behave. Without the benefit of growing up in a nurturing environment with supportive relationships, long-term exposure to trauma can cause what is called toxic stress. Yes, children can be stressed out!

Toxic stress is defined as prolonged, severe, and chronic, with negative consequences affecting the mind and body. We can see how Mariah, after being in a constant state of emotional trauma without relief throughout childhood, would have problems coping.

During college, she medicated herself with alcohol and participated in promiscuous activities, which may have been her unconscious way of coping. Adults who experience traumatic events with a lack of affection as children respond to life differently. They may suffer from emotional issues such as depression and anxiety. Without the supportive relationships of family, a teacher, or any of the other people who surrounded her in life, Mariah also suffered from depression throughout her life.

Is There Hope for Mariah

I found that healthcare providers have developed an approach to healing that would benefit Miriah. The approach is called Trauma-Informed Care, and it is care used by trained healthcare professionals designed to take a holistic approach to treatment. This approach involves looking at what has happened in a person's life in the past and present to create a plan for healing. A few things Trauma care consists of are realizing, recognizing, responding, and resisting re-traumatization.

Some of the principles for trauma care are safety, trustworthiness, and peer support. The use of these principles demonstrates to me that Mariah will gain some healing from exposure to this approach.

Part One Summary

In Part One, we discussed the meaning of trauma and nurture. The fictional story of Mariah's life experiences helps us to understand how and why she became the type of adult she ultimately became. We also looked at some of the brain science and psychology of what happens when children are traumatized and unnurtured. Mariah's story did not end without hope. Findings show that trauma-informed healthcare approaches are being conducted and receiving support at the State and Federal levels.

I find it comforting to know and share with you the realization that decades of brain research on the effects of trauma are being utilized to make an essential difference in the lives of children and adults. The understanding of the importance of nurture in developing healthy minds and bodies of children is being recognized as critical and is not overlooked.

As we conclude part one, I am confident that, with the understanding and approach provided here, childcare providers, parents, family members, guardians, and all in the community who interact with young children will be empowered to nurture each child into adulthood.

A Brief Note About Part Two

In Part Two, Children are referred to as flowers in a flower garden because they have a lot in common with flowers: To bloom, they must be adequately nurtured; they all have different needs, and their differences make each one more beautiful. As an addition to Part One, Part Two reinforces the second edition of Nurture as it zeroes in on nurturing the social, emotional, and cognitive needs of children and explains how to promote the importance of play, encourage children to develop trusting relationships, guide and discipline, and share activities that support learning in a nurturing environment.

The following is a nurturing approach to trauma with biblical guidance. Each letter that spells "Nurture" is used in conjunction with biblical scriptures to define and provide a deeper meaning to its importance.

Dr. Mattie Lee Jones

Nurturing With Biblical Guidance

2 Timothy 3:16 All Scripture is inspired by God and beneficial for teaching, for rebuke, for correction, for training in righteousness.

N	nourishing	To do or provide what's needed for someone to be healthy and to grow and develop strongly	Isaiah 40:29 He gives strength to the weary, And to him who lacks might He increases power.
U	unconditional Love	A love that is given, and despite what a person does; it is never completely withdrawn	1 John 4:16 And we have known and believed in the love that God hath for us. God is love, and he that dwelleth in love dwelleth in God and God in him.
R	raise	To take care of a person, or an animal or plant, until they are completely grown	Proverbs 22:6 Train up a child in the way he should go, Even when he is old he will not depart from it.
T	trust	To believe that someone is good and honest and will not harm you, or that something is safe and reliable	Isaiah 12:2 "Behold, God is my salvation, I will trust and not be afraid; For the Lord God is my strength and song, And He has become my salvation."
U	uplifting	Positive in a way that encourages the improvement of a person's mood or spirit. Words are powerful; may build or destroy a person	Ephesians 4:29 Let no unwholesome word proceed from your mouth, but only such a word as is good for edification according to the need of the moment, so that it will give grace to those who hear.

R	resilient	Able to withstand or recover quickly from difficult conditions. Resilience is learned from examples of others in our lives.	2 Timothy 1:5 (letter from Paul to Timothy) "having been reminded of the unfeigned faith that is in thee; which dwelt first in thy grandmother Lois, and thy mother Eunice; and, I am persuaded, in thee also."
E	encouragement	Words or behavior that give someone the confidence to do something	Ephesians 6:4 Fathers, do not provoke your children to anger, but bring them up in the discipline and instruction of the Lord.

Sources:

https://bible.knowing-jesus.com/topics/Nurture

https://bible.knowing-jesus.com/phrases/God-is-Love

https://dictionary.cambridge.org/dictionary/english

https://bible.knowing-jesus.com/topics

PART TWO

Introduction

NURTURE

Connecting the Social, Emotional, and Cognitive Needs of Children

My reflections of children are like beautiful flowers in a garden. An expert gardener knows plants must be adequately nurtured to grow and flower to their full potential. Each variety of flower may have different needs, but their differences make the garden so beautiful. Thus, it is with children; they are each uniquely different and beautiful.

An expert gardener knows plants must be nurtured appropriately to grow and flower to their full potential. Various flowers may have different needs, but their differences make the garden beautiful. Nurture is an action word. The dictionary defines it as the act or process of promoting a child's development, something that nourishes, feeds, protects, supports, and encourages.

For example, to become successful gardeners, the gardener (caregiver) must be willing to put time and effort into nurturing the growth of each flower variety.

I love roses; they are one of my favorite flowers. They come in many colors and varieties. I have tried many times to grow roses, but the experience has been challenging. I planted roses with a purple tint, but the rose bush did not grow. I tried another orange variety, but it soon died. Finally, I tried a red rose bush, which survived for two seasons and became unproductive. I could not understand why I was not successful growing this beautiful flower I loved.

I soon realized that I did not know what I was doing. I had to do some research to learn how to grow roses successfully. The American Rose Society (ARS) provides information by rosarians (experts on roses). From the information on their website, I found there were many things I needed to consider to become successful in growing roses.

I also found research beneficial as I endeavored to gain knowledge and expertise about children's developmental needs. I had the opportunity to visit many child-care facilities to observe interactions and relationships between adults and the children in their care. I obtained parents' perspectives by visiting homes and meeting them at restaurants, their children's activities, or sports events. Documenting my observations of child-care facilities and conversations with parents allowed me to share my expertise in early childhood education.

I have shared my perspectives in the four books I have written, which cover the following areas: parents' perspectives concerning their children's educational process; parents' personal experiences and how they affect their parenting; a guide for child-care providers on guidance for young children (discipline); and nurturing ways to connect the social, emotional, and cognitive development of children. Some excerpts from my previous books are included in Nurture.

As a presenter and trainer of early childhood education students and workers, I support the premise that healthy adult relationships are essential in nurturing young children. My previous service on the Indiana Association for the Education of Young Children (IAEYC) board as the chair of the Professional Development Committee allows me to play a vital role in advising the professional development needs of child-care workers and providers.

Many resource websites, such as the National Association for the Education of Young Children (NAEYC), which I am a member, provide research and articles by experts about young children.

Children encompass many diversities and cultures. They are not only beautiful but also our most valuable asset. Nothing is more worthy of our investment.

Research shows that to create a nurturing experience for children, three areas of development—social, emotional, and cognitive—must be connected. I have found throughout my observations that most preschools have the appropriate cognitive curriculum but lose sight of the importance of guiding children socially and emotionally. For example, a child who is not taught how to self-regulate (emotional) or get along with his peers (social) will have a gap in his cognitive development that can manifest as discipline issues. Connecting these three areas of child development is crucial in understanding and interacting with the world around them.

Nurture discusses each area of child development and merges them to show how children's development is connected to their experiences and interactions with adults and peers.

Nurture goes further by revealing the importance of these developmental connections as they are defined, using the comparison of a child's healthy mind, body, and spirit. Finally, steps for working together to create a nurturing preschool environment for children are demonstrated and shared.

Nurturing the Social Development of Children

Children are all beautiful. Their differences come from genetics and the situations they are exposed to socially, emotionally, and cognitively. As they grow and develop, exposure becomes the ground that nurtures or depletes them. It is vital to encourage children appropriately from infancy.

Crucial brain development happens in a child's early years (birth to three years). Children learn to express themselves and gain confidence and creativity during this time. A nurturing learning environment engages children socially, emotionally, and cognitively.

The Role of Play

Playtime is critical to nurturing children's social development, and its value cannot be underestimated. Children are exposed to many learning and developmentally necessary peer interactions during play. Nurturing guidance is crucial at playtime because children develop in areas that prepare them for adolescence, teen years, and adulthood.

The following is an excerpt from my book Disciplining Someone Else's Children (2015), which examines the role of play in the development of young children. Understanding a child's developmental progress is essential for understanding, accepting, or correcting his/her behavior (as well as the teacher's response). Remember, children have differences in temperament, development, and behavior.

An essential part of discipline is knowing whether to intervene or let children be children. Safety is the priority, and danger needs immediate action. The child-care providers are responsible for teaching children, directly or indirectly. This may mean stopping or redirecting a child's undesirable behavior for their safety or the safety of other children.

During my visits to several child-care providers' facilities, I Observed that many teachers faced challenging behaviors during playtime. Often, the teacher's frustration could have been avoided by understanding what children are experiencing developmentally during play. A website article by Child Action Inc. titled "The Importance of Play" revealed that children's play behavior develops in stages. "Play allows children to explore new things at their own pace, master physical ability, learn new skills, and figure things out in their way."

Children learn leadership skills During play with others by directing the action or following a leader. The typical stages of onlooker behavior are watching what other children do but not joining in the play. Solitary play: playing alone without regard for others; being involved in independent activities, like art or playing with blocks or other materials. Parallel activity: playing near others but not interacting, even using the same play materials. Associative play: playing in small groups with no definite rules or assigned roles, and cooperative play is deciding to work together to complete a building project or pretend to play with assigned roles for all the members of the group of children.

Learning to share is a process that takes several years to develop. Children will need proper adult supervision to master this skill. If children do not master this skill, their reactions could cause discipline concerns. The article by Child Action also defined the following three stages of development in learning to share, the first stage being that children think everything is "mine." The second stage is when children discover that some things belong to others. The third stage is when children know they can lend and get a toy back. Children are more likely to share when they see their toys come back to them and when other children share with their toys.

Play is not just a pastime for children; it is a crucial learning environment that enhances their social competence and emotional maturity. According to Smilansky and Shefatya (1990), a child's success in school is heavily influenced by their ability to interact positively with peers and adults. Therefore, play is a vital component of a child's social development.

Play is a powerful tool for emotional development, providing children with a means to express and manage their feelings (Jalongo, April 2014). The significance of play in children's lives is well-documented. Their play also evolves as children mature, following a distinct developmental sequence.

Playtime is a necessary learning environment for children. Teachers should use this time to teach children many valuable social skills. Some preschoolers may have tantrums. Their tantrums, however, should not be as severe as those of a two-year-old because they should be gaining more control over their emotions. They also display aggressive behavior but should learn to use their words instead of their impulses.

Teachers should be concerned when children exhibit behaviors that professionals consider outside of normal misbehavior, such as psychological behaviors that impair their ability to function. It is usual for preschoolers to try to gain more independence. For example, they may argue and exercise their right to say no. Preschoolers also want to have the freedom of older children while still craving attention like a baby. Some warning signs of abnormal behavior on the American Academy of Pediatrics website are Difficulty managing emotional outbursts, difficulty managing impulses (such as physical aggression and verbal impulses), and behavior that does not respond to discipline.

It is usual for children to repeat misbehavior from time to time. They do this to see if the care provider will follow through with discipline. Abnormal behavior, however, may include misbehavior that does not respond to appropriate disciplinary action, behavior that interferes with school and causes a child to fall behind academically, and behavior that interferes with social interactions.

Rosarians say that one essential aspect of successfully growing roses is being consistent with their care and nurturing. Consistency is also essential in the social development of children.

Self-Image

Each child is a unique individual. Babies have personalities, likes and dislikes, and, yes, characters. Babies must be exposed to a consistent and loving environment to support a healthy, positive self-image. Caring relationships are key. Children learn to love by being loved. Knowing each baby's character means learning to recognize what they respond to, such as sounds and facial expressions.

My daughter was a sensitive baby. She would tear up if I looked at her with a sad face, but my happy face made her smile. From toddler to teenage years, she did not like seeing me look unhappy or disappointed. Knowing her character helped me determine how to respond to her when she needed correction and support. For example, since my daughter was sensitive to my feelings and was hurt whenever she felt that I was disappointed in her, I realized that she was a child who did not need to be spanked. I could redirect and guide her without being physical.

Babies' eyes open soon after birth, and from that point on, they watch their surroundings, especially those of their caregivers (parents and guardians). From birth, they are developing a sense of self. Their surroundings and interactions will negatively or positively affect how they view themselves as children and into adulthood. Toddlers watch the reactions and responses they get from the things they do. They also view themselves by the way they are treated. Positive or negative caregivers play a role in molding the self-image of children.

In my book What Did Your Parents Do to You, I share how outside influences that are out of control, such as bullying, peer pressure, and other adult contacts (teachers, relatives), shape children and how they react to life. (I defined parents as anyone legally responsible for the care of a child and those with whom the child lives.).

I have heard many stories in the more than twenty years I have talked to parents about children as an educator, school principal, and parenting trainer. I find it interesting to listen to parents reflect on their childhoods when dealing with their children. Parents have told me how they hated certain things their parents did to them, but they did the same to their children.

Children's responses to interactions with their surroundings are unique, and their influence on their character is equally exceptional. It is said that dysfunction has become acceptable in our society, so much so that it has been given labels and reenacted on television as entertainment. Sitcoms, cartoons, and reality television profile dysfunctional situations. Some sitcoms portray the dysfunctional relationship between teachers and children in a classroom situation as entertainment.

Webster's Dictionary defines dysfunctional as "impaired to function." Impaired is to "make worse; to diminish in quality, value, excellence, and strength; to deteriorate." This definition leaves me pondering what type of deteriorating effect dysfunction has on children. In one of his sermons, a well-known pastor and author discussed how painful it is to get adulthood, which you should have gotten as a child. Sometimes, children have both a negative and positive relationship with their caregivers—the kind of negative, hurtful experience that leaves them feeling unloved, mixed with positive experiences that make them feel that their caregivers do care and love them. These mixed, inconsistent interactions can confuse their childhood and adult lives.

Can we stop the cycle of damaging the self-images of

children? I discerned the following from many conversations with adults (who shared their stories in my book What Did Your Parents Do to You): when a child is abused or mistreated, they may grow up to abuse and hate. As adults, they may hate what they are doing but cannot change their behavior. They may not realize that they are reacting to what happened to them in the past. Many children who survive bad experiences never tell anyone what they went through.

As adults, some say they do not feel that anyone would understand or believe them. They internalize the experience and let it define who they are. It is challenging for a child to understand how those who are supposed to love and keep them safe can do the opposite. When children who have been mistreated act negatively, they are misunderstood and are thought to be solely to blame. These actions include fighting in elementary school, drug and alcohol abuse in high school, and sexual abuse as an adult. Many of these actions are a result of having a poor self-image.

In her book What I Know for Sure, Oprah Winfrey shared that some of the things she experienced as a youth caused her to feel unworthy, and healing the wounds of the past was tremendous but worthwhile. She wrote, "I know that healing the wounds of the past is one of life's biggest and worthwhile challenges. It is important to know when and how you were programmed so you can change the program."

When a garden does not receive proper nurturing, the flowers' appearance (image) is affected. Studies show that when children are not adequately nurtured at school and home, their self-images can be negatively affected. Positive nurturing can transform a negative self-image, such as intervention, support, and love.

Expression

Flowering plants flourish and blossom in the appropriate environment, which includes the right amount of sunshine, water, and care. Children thrive when nurtured in a safe, caring learning environment where they are loved and respected. When children feel safe to express what they want and feel, they blossom from young children into teenagers and adults in a positive way.

As an artist, I enjoy watching children express themselves through artistic means, such as coloring, drawing, and writing. These processes help children develop communication skills and social expression, which allows them to show the world who they are in ways that cannot be put into words.

I have read many articles written by psychology expert Kendra Cherry. In the article "What is Art, (2016), she stated that as an expressive medium, art can be used to communicate, overcome stress (children can and do experience levels of stress), and explore different aspects of one's personality.

The American Art Therapy Association describes

art therapy as a process that can enhance individuals of all ages' mental and emotional well-being. Art is also described as a toddler's first visual language. As stated earlier, children express themselves during playtime. They also learn cooperation, relationship skills, and respect for others. Caregivers should allow children to express themselves freely during play while keeping them safe and using playtime for teachable moments.

Give toddlers objects with which they can build using their imaginations. They learn to develop by following verbal or written instructions as they reach school age. This activity makes them aware of the importance of guidelines.

Children express themselves uniquely differently from birth as they connect to their surroundings. Babies respond to their surroundings before they are born. As babies, they see, feel, taste, and begin to communicate by responding in ways that become expressions of who they are. As we pay attention to their responses to stimuli, such as noises, tone of voice, and facial expressions of others, we get to know their likes and dislikes. For instance, my daughter would get very disturbed if she heard yelling. I used this as a cue when interacting with her.

As children connect to their surroundings, they learn to focus and have self-control. Babies' reactions to stimuli and how they express themselves differ for each child. Author and leading child development expert Ellen Galinsky shared information on how infants connect to their surroundings in her book Mind in the Making. She notes that if we adults could find ways to relate to what babies are doing, we could understand what they are experiencing. We can gain this understanding by paying attention to the positive and negative ways the baby reacts to stimulation; then, we can respond in a nurturing way.

Learning to Trust

As a component of my inquiry into children's relationships with their caregivers, I observed that preschool children learn best when teachers develop positive and caring relationships. A nurturing teacher gains the trust of children more instinctively. Research shows that children learn best in safe, trusting learning environments and respond positively when receiving age-appropriate, carefully planned guidance and assistance.

Age-appropriate strategies nurture children at each age and stage of development. Preschool children have begun to develop understanding and brain readiness from their experiences, activities, and interactions. The following is a reflection from my book Disciplining Someone Else's Children (2015).

Developing a trusting relationship with preschool children is essential to their emotional and social growth. I also have discerned that it is just as crucial for child-care workers (director, teacher, teacher assistant, etc.) to gain the children's trust in their care as it is for the children to trust their parents. Child-care workers have a responsibility to initiate and develop this trusting relationship.

A trusting relationship can be developed and maintained by providing children with opportunities, letting them know they are cared for and safe, and treating them with respect. The way to empower children is by allowing them to explore their interests and try new things. The teacher's role is to ensure their safety while they engage in these activities. This approach builds trust and fosters a sense of empowerment in children.

I have observed that teachers creating a safe classroom learning environment are often more relaxed. They are comfortable allowing children to make their own choices from the activities or workstations in the classroom, such as dramatic play or manipulative stations. This allows the children to feel that the teacher trusts them and is willing to let them learn independently.

As the teacher monitors the children, he or she is confident that even if a child gets in trouble, this can be a healthy learning experience or even a teachable moment. Children need and want to know that they are essential.

Children learn to trust when teachers tell them they care about them, no matter what—even if they get in trouble.

When redirecting or stopping undesirable behavior, the teacher can demonstrate that they care about the child by giving the child a task to do, such as letting the child be a helper for the day. This sends the message, "I do not care for your behavior, but I do care about you." "Let yes mean yes, and no mean no." You may have heard this saying before, but it is essential when communicating with young children. Being consistent with responses is the key. Preschool children will respond to expectations because they want to please. The rules should not change daily, depending on the teacher's mood.

Children should know what to expect, even if they get into trouble. When undesirable behavior has a consequence, the consequence should be communicated clearly and carried out. Yes, even carrying out a consequence builds trust. Consequences are to correct undesirable behavior, not "threats."

When promises are kept, and a trusting relationship is established, preschool children demonstrate remarkable resilience. They bounce back easier and quicker from adverse and challenging situations, reinforcing the positive impact of trust on their development.

It is imperative to their children's social-emotional development that parents support their child-care providers' efforts to correct undesirable and disruptive behavior. They have to be on the same page to get appropriate results.

Young children need the help of loving parents and child-care providers to develop strong, secure, trusting, bonding relationships during the infant years through age three. If they develop correctly, the independence they want as toddlers will be balanced. When they become preschool age, however, they will continue to need the support of parents and their child-care provider to build more and more confidence and trust in themselves.

Children's social contact with adults also provides the stimulation and experience their brains need to develop healthily. The love shown to children through how they are touched can send positive, soothing messages that make them feel loved and special. This social growth is paired with emotional development as they gain resilience, self-regulation, and trusting relationships.

Advances in brain research show how the brain

continues to grow and develop after birth. It has been demonstrated that the growth of the brain is not only determined by genetics; it is also dependent upon the child's experiences. Interactions with other people and objects are vital for brain growth, as food nourishes the body. As stated earlier, as children grow and mature, their ability to become socially and emotionally healthy will be affected by their relationships.

While positive early experiences help the brain to develop well, negative experiences, such as neglect and abuse, can cause some genetically normal children to have mental disorders or develop serious emotional problems. Supporting information found in the article "Facts for Life: Child Development & Early Learning Facts" highlighted that each time a child uses any of the five senses, a neural connection is made in the brain. As the child repeats using the senses, new connections are made that shape the way the child thinks, feels, behaves, and learns, which gives evidence that a close, nurturing relationship with child-care workers is a way to nourish a child's growing brain.

Nurturing the Emotional Development of Children

As an American Rose Society rosarian once said, roses strongly desire to grow, often overcoming most technique deficiencies. Similarly, humans, from infancy to toddlers and toddlers to school age, have an innate drive to grow. However, the quality of this growth, or development, is heavily influenced by the knowledge and actions of their caregivers (parents, guardians, child-care providers, and teachers). This underscores the crucial role of caregivers in fostering emotional development.

They absorb their surroundings. Children will model how they are treated and what they see and repeat what is heard. For this reason, caregivers must not be afraid to give and show love to children. Children need unconditional love.

The definition of unconditional love is affection without limits or conditions, complete love. The Bible says that God loves us unconditionally—what a wonderful gift. It is also noted that children learn to love by being loved. Through my research for the book What Did Your Parents Do to You, I met many adults who grew up never knowing what it meant to be loved unconditionally. It is not easy to share an experience with a child you did not experience yourself.

Love is an essential key to nurturing a child to be healthy emotionally.

A child who is developing healthily will have positive social and emotional responses to life through resilience, self-regulation, and forming relationships.

Resilience

Resurgence & Ecologist magazine chose a flower for the cover of their November–December 2009 issue to illustrate "resilience."

Blossoms and flowers are resilient; they stand out there in the wind, in the rain, in the snow, in the sunshine—day and night—unperturbed, undiminished. They are resilient because they are flexible and fragrant, pliable and pleasant, supple and soft, tender and tolerant, gentle, adaptable, and light.

Bing dictionary defines resilience as "speedy recovery from problems: the ability to recover quickly from setbacks. Elasticity: the ability of matter to spring back quickly into shape after being bent, stretched, or deformed." Caregivers should be aware of the importance of teaching children to be resilient—to bounce back—and should not assume that resilience happens. This ability is essential for survival.

Individuals and communities can rebuild their lives with resilience, even after devastating tragedies. During times of tragedy, adults are in survival mode, and resilience is not what they think of when considering children. Unintentionally, adults may not stop to ensure that children learn from whatever has happened.

Children are not born with resilience; they develop resilience as they grow up and gain better thinking, self-management skills, and knowledge. Older counterparts. Depression can play a role, but among the youngest suicides, a predisposition to impulsiveness is just as important. Children who kill themselves often have a mood disorder, ADHD, or a "conduct disorder," which means antisocial behavior.

Living in an abusive household can lay the groundwork for suicidal behavior, and an incident like getting kicked out of school or a dying relative can trigger it. Bully-related suicide can be connected to any type of bullying, including physical bullying, emotional bullying, cyberbullying, and "sexting" or circulating suggestive or nude photos or messages about a person.

A few years ago, I read an article about a six-year-old boy who committed suicide because he was upset over his parents' divorce. Being resilient does not mean going through life without experiencing stress and pain. People feel grief, sadness, and other emotions after adversity and loss. The road to resilience lies in working through the feelings and effects of stress and painful events.

What has happened that a child comes to the point where there is no hope? How can adults set an example of resilience for the children in their care? We cannot say, "They are young; they will get over whatever situation is causing them distress." Factors contributing to resilience include close relationships with family and friends, a positive view of self, confidence in personal strengths and abilities, and the ability to manage strong feelings and impulses.

According to Edith H. Grothberg, parents' and other caregivers' responses to situations are models for children. Their help in a child's response is vital because their response will both promote and inhibit resilience. Many say that adults and children share the same indications of resilience, such as the ability to relate to other children and adults, bounce back after a negative interaction, courage, and laughter.

Child caregivers should know and look for signs of resilience in the children they have in their care so that they can provide teaching, support, and intervention. Resilience also plays a vital role in a child's ability to self-regulate.

Self-Regulation

Socially, children learn to respond and relate to their peers and adults healthily. Emotionally, they learn to self-regulate and have self-control. Helping children develop self-regulation skills is similar to helping children learn to read and write. Nurturing teachers use various strategies to connect children who learn socially and emotionally to more complex skills and knowledge. Three teaching strategies critical to children's development of self-regulation are modeling, using hints and cues, and gradually withdrawing adult support.

Self-regulation is not an isolated skill. Children must translate what they experience into information they can use to regulate thoughts, emotions, and behaviors (Blair & Diamond, 2008). For example, infants may translate the feel of a soothing touch and the sound of soft voices into cues that help them develop self-calming skills.

Toddlers and preschoolers begin to translate cues from adults—such as "Your turn is next"—into regulation that helps them inhibit urges to grab food or toys. They learn how long they must usually wait to be served food or to have a turn playing with a desired toy rather than just grabbing it, which also helps them regulate emotional tension. Research shows that emotional regulation connects with every aspect of a child's developmental well-being (Bell & Wolfe, 2014).

Self-regulation has been compared to using a thermostat because both are active, intentional processes. Setting a thermostat requires deliberate decision-making, and the device actively monitors environmental temperature. Similarly, self-regulation requires the child to make intentional decisions and engage in active processes.

Although many processes outside their awareness regulate children's behavior, researchers have found that children's intentional self-regulation predicts school success (Zimmerman, 1994). When provided with appropriate opportunities, young children can learn intentional self-regulation. Researchers found that planning helped children develop more vital self-regulation skills (Bodrova & Leong 2007).

Planning is an integral part of self-regulation. Children's regulatory skills become more sophisticated (Kopp, 1982; Blair & Diamond, 2008). Studies show that infants begin to regulate arousal and sensory-motor responses before birth. An infant may suck her thumb after hearing a loud sound, indicating that she is regulating her response to the environment.

Toddlers start to inhibit responses and comply with adult caregivers. Children exhibit more complex forms of self-regulation by age four, such as anticipating appropriate responses and modifying their responses when circumstances are subtly different. For example, clapping is appropriate after someone speaks during sharing time at school but not while a teacher gives directions.

Self-regulation skills develop gradually, so adults must hold developmentally appropriate expectations for children's behavior. Adults create routines to help manage and guide children; if these routines are consistent, they also help children self-regulate. Consistent routines involve activities at about the same time and in the same way each day.

During my observations at several child-care facilities, I noticed that most teachers had a daily morning routine. During the morning routines, the children appeared comfortable and displayed a sense of emotional security.

Routines also provide an opportunity for the teacher to model behavior for children. By demonstrating appropriate behavior, teachers show children how to accomplish a task and use the self-regulation skills needed to complete the task.

Child-care experts say that routines help children learn to trust that the adults in their lives will provide what the children need. This trust gives children the freedom to play, explore, and learn. Children's social skills are essential to their cognitive development. Children who develop positive social skills like self-regulation transition more successfully at school and reach academic achievement (Ladd, Birch 1996).

As mentioned earlier, loving and caring relationships make the connections that babies need to get to know the world and their places in it. The way that young children are treated and the experiences they have, both positive and negative, form the reference they will use throughout the rest of their lives. Relationships guide children as they develop socially and emotionally, which includes the ability to play, communicate, learn, face challenges (resilience), and emotionally regulate (self-regulation).

Children need trusting relationships to develop empathy, compassion, sharing, and well-being. Children must form secure relationships that allow them to explore and learn if they are to thrive.

Children experience their world through the relationships and interactions they have with adults. This relationship must be safe, stable, and nurturing. "Essentials for Childhood: Steps to Create Safe, Stable, Nurturing Relationships & Environments for All Children," published by the Center for Injury Prevention and Control (CDC) 2014, documented findings that confirm that three critical qualities that make a difference for children as they grow.

These three qualities also shape children's physical, emotional, social, and cognitive development, affecting their health as adults. These qualities are as follows: Safety—the extent to which a child is free from fear and secure from physical or psychological harm within their social and physical environment. Stability—the degree of predictability and consistency in a child's social, emotional, and physical environment. Nurturing—the extent to which a parent or caregiver is available and able to sensitively and consistently respond to and meet the needs of the child

As a school administrator, I learned a lot from the large Hispanic culture in one of the schools I was assigned to serve. I researched to understand Hispanic culture better, which increased my awareness of communicating better with parents and their children. I was able to nurture the children more meaningfully. When caregivers respect a child's culture, they gain their parents' and children's trust.

I also found that the type of relationship and interaction children have with adults is influenced by their culture. The culture in which children develop dramatically influences how they respond to the world around them. Culture, such as fundamental beliefs and values, affects a child's daily routine. How a child's parents' culture displays love and compassion will affect how the child is nurtured and disciplined.

Discipline is vital to providing a nurturing environment for children of all ages. A nurturing environment that is conducive to learning does not tolerate disruptive behavior. This guidance is used as a way to teach and is administered in a consistent, nurturing, and loving way.

Childcare providers should depend on their understanding of children's social and emotional development to correct unwanted behavior. To guide prevention and intervention in child development, childcare providers may use professional development tools, such as the book Disciplining Someone Else's Children, which I wrote in 2015. The following is an excerpt from this book.

Strategies for disciplining young children have gained many descriptions, such as classroom management, setting limits, setting boundaries, redirection, teaching self-control, and teachable moments. The Merriam-Webster Dictionary defines discipline as control that is gained by requiring that rules or orders be obeyed and punishing bad behavior, as well as a way of behaving that shows a willingness to obey rules or orders.

The discipline policies childcare providers use should be clear and shared with parents with many questions and concerns.

Regarding discipline, there should be collaboration with childcare providers who influence actions taken at home to correct behavior. Childcare providers have shared with me that their efforts to correct unwanted behavior are unsuccessful when parents do not set the exact expectations in the home.

One alarming concern today is the suspensions and expulsions of young children from child-care facilities. Suspension is an extreme disciplinary action because the child is removed from the learning environment for a short or long period. Expulsions are used in some cases, meaning the child is removed permanently. Does this type of discipline work?

In Disciplining Someone Else's Children, I shared an interview I conducted with a director of a child-care facility with over two hundred children. In the following, suspension of young children is the focus of my interview with the child-care facility director.

Interview with a Child-Care Facility Director

Dr. Jones: Director Carey, what age group of children have you had to suspend from your childcare?

Director: The youngest child was aged two. Children are suspended mostly because of continual fighting with the other children or when we cannot get the parents to help with the situation. Some children bit when they fought with the other children. One of the discipline rules of our facility is three bites, and you are suspended.

We gave one child more than three chances to change her behavior. This child bit up to ten times. We suspended the child for two days.

Dr. Jones: How did the parents react to the child being suspended?

Director: They were upset but not surprised because we had given them plenty of warnings about the child biting and fighting.

Dr. Jones: Did the suspension change the child's behavior?

Director: No, not really. When the child came back, the biting and fighting continued. We realize that biting is an issue with some two-year-olds, but children who are three and still biting become a concern.

Dr. Jones: Does suspension work, in your opinion?

Director: Suspension sometimes works. For example, one child hit a teacher and threw toys. The child was suspended for a day, returned, and was calm for about a week, but then went through the same behavior and suspension process again.

Dr. Jones: As the director, what role do you play in the decision to suspend a child?

Director: In most cases, the teacher will call for me to get the child acting out of control in a classroom. I will get the child out of the room and take him or her to my office.

Parents are then called and given directions to get the child immediately. About 80 percent of the parents will or can come immediately. Some children have to sit in my office to wait for them.

When children become so out of control that no redirection or discipline will correct or stop the behavior, parents are usually asked to take them home for the day.

Extreme situations cause the child to be suspended for extended periods, such as biting or throwing things at the teacher or other children.

Dr. Jones: What is the cause of children getting out of control?

Director: I have found that most children want to please their teachers. They act out when they have not bonded with them or do not feel like the teacher cares about them.

When I go to the classroom to retrieve a child, the teacher calls me to remove it. The first thing I try to do is hug the child. I hug him, love on him, and comfort him. The child will respond positively because she trusts me. I often get her to return to the classroom without any other incident that day.

I have loved the child, which has settled him or her down. I try to be an example. Some teachers get it; some do not.

I have not seen evidence that suspensions work. They seem to relieve the teacher of a child's aggressiveness out of control for whatever reason.

We will suspend children permanently if they are a danger to themselves or others. I love them all and do not like suspending our children.

Reflection after the Interview with the Child-Care Director

In my experience, most child-care directors use suspension as a last alternative to correcting behavior. This action is usually taken to get parents' attention and make them aware of their problems with a child. This action may also show the other children that certain behaviors will not be tolerated.

From my perspective on the suspension of young children, I first noticed a facial expression that revealed a sense of dismay as they shared the instances that led them to determine that suspension was necessary. I found that they are very much aware that children need to be in a safe learning environment and that suspending them may be taking them away from what they need.

They tell me that the safety needs of all the children

in their care must be considered. It is for this reason that they do what is necessary. They hope parents understand and the children learn they love them, but certain behaviors are not conducive to learning and will not be tolerated.

Disciplining young children requires clarification because it can have damaging effects if not administered correctly. Some child-care providers clarify how they discipline by providing a policy shared with child-care workers and parents. The discipline policy clarifies the appropriate responses to misbehavior—those that should not be done under any circumstance and those that are acceptable.

Having spent extensive time in various child-care facilities, closely observing the dynamics between teachers and children, I can see that teachers often struggle with managing disruptive behavior. They seem to grasp the skills for delivering an age-appropriate curriculum more swiftly than those needed to handle disruptive children.

The Merriam-Webster Dictionary defines prevention as the act or practice of stopping something wrong from happening; the act of preventing or hindering. It defines intervention as intervening to become involved in something (such as a conflict) to influence what happens. I feel that childcare providers have one of the most essential jobs globally. They are responsible for our world's most valuable asset—our children. As the child's first teacher, they work in collaboration with parents.

Research has shown that the first years leave a lasting impression on children's lives. Child-care facilities focus on children's cognitive, social, and emotional development in daily routines and activities. Discipline is a part of children's social and emotional development and can hinder their progress if not addressed appropriately.

To successfully nurture children in this area, teachers and other child-care workers should use strategies that answer the following questions:

- How do you prevent disruptive behavior that interrupts other children's learning?
- How do you intervene to stop disruptive behavior from getting out of control and becoming damaging to the other children in your care?

Instilling discipline in children is a pivotal aspect of their holistic development. How can childcare providers ensure they make the right choices in this crucial area of child development? Disciplining someone else's children is a daily responsibility of a childcare teacher and a vital part of fostering a safe learning environment for all children.

Remember that each child is unique and develops at his or her rate. Mental, developmental, and exceptional-needs issues may also require additional specialized guidance.

During my visits to child-care facilities, I observed that many teachers tended to use the same discipline actions repeatedly, whether it worked previously or not. They seemed to do this during times when they allowed themselves to become frustrated. Some of the actions I observed teachers use are as follows: Threatening to take away an activity they know the child enjoys (e.g., recess), yelling out the child's name over and over, and saying things that are meant to shame the child or make him or her feel guilty. They involved the other children in the classroom by using the child as an example of wrong or harmful behavior.

In the health article "It is Not Discipline—It is a Teachable Moment," author Tara Parker-Pope quoted Dr. Ginsburg's statement, "It is not about punishment. It is about teaching that changes things." When discipline is used as punishment, teachers lose the opportunity to teach.

Certain situations with children that escalate into a child's being disciplined (punished) could have been prevented. Children learn to manage their emotions and relationships at each age and stage of development. They must experience many life events and situations to learn to do this. Child-care providers' responsibility is to understand and nurture them through these situations.

Both "spoiled" and harshly disciplined children are at risk for emotional and behavioral problems. Being consistent in the approach or discipline strategy can change the course of the child's development. Children's age and stage of development determine their emotional responses. Keeping this in mind, what might be seen as misbehaving may be a necessary teachable moment for the child.

An example would be a two-year-old upset or unhappy because a toy he or she favored was taken away (this is a normal response for a toddler). A caregiver aware of a child's age and stage of development would use this understanding to teach the child how to handle the emotion and move on (transition).

For more information and resources on developmentally appropriate practice (DAP), visit the National Association for the Education of Young Children website at naeyc.org/DAP.

Nurturing the Cognitive Development of Children

I will define a beautiful garden as having many flowers of different shapes, colors, and fragrances. Each specimen of flower grows at specified rates. The gardener has to consider the whole plant as it develops from a seed or bulb into what it was designed to be. In comparison, for a child to develop cognitively adequately, the whole child must be considered.

My studies revealed that children develop cognitively

as they develop socially and emotionally. Part 3 will consider how children's social and emotional development plays a vital role in connecting to children's cognitive needs (learning processes).

Their uniqueness must also be considered to nurture children to their full potential. Two of these unique areas include character and level of mental readiness. Brain research shows that children are ready to learn specific cognitive skills at different ages and levels of mental development. For this reason, if learning is to take place, activities must be precise and appropriate and accommodate the level at which children are mentally ready to learn.

As children grow and develop, they also reach milestones—the actions most children can do by a certain age, such as crawling or drawing. Advances in brain research confirm that children begin to learn the moment they are born. The first years of life impact the success they will experience at school age.

As described in the article "Memory and the Brain" on the website The Human Memory (www.human-memory.net/brain_neurons.html), early experiences that are nurturing create a brain with more neuron structures that determine intelligence and behavior.

Children grow tremendously in all three areas of development during the first three years of life. A newborn's brain is about 25 percent of its adult weight. By age three, the brain has produced billions of cells and hundreds of trillions of connections, or synapses, between these cells. The Human Memory website defines

Synapses are the brain's memory. The central nervous system's core and brain components are the neuron—a nerve cell, "the brain cells" of popular language. This critical brain development demonstrates the need to understand how learning is stimulated in children.

How Children Learn

As stated earlier, studies show that children learn from the surroundings, actions, and reactions of others, such as parents, relatives, other children, and teachers. This learning from others comes during play and everyday experiences. Children also learn from verbal and nonverbal communication. Language and conversation (talking) are learned from listening and repeating what they hear. I find it fascinating that children can learn more than one language from birth.

Bruce Perry, MD, PhD, in his article "How Children Learn Language," stated, "In the first years of life, children listen, practice, and learn." He indicated no genetic code leads a child to speak English, Spanish, or Japanese. Language is learned; humans are born with the ability to make up to forty different sounds, and genetically, our brains can make associations between sounds and objects, actions, or ideals. This natural language learning process should reassure you about your child's development. Combined, these abilities allow language creation, and through this process, sound has meaning.

Research by Tamar Kushnir, "Learning about How Children Learn," 2009, shed light on how children learn through everyday experiences. Her findings show that children display psychological intuition. Children achieve this by observing the actions of other human beings and then by concluding the underlying reason they do what they do. She found that children also ascertain the motivations, desires, and preferences that are displayed during the actions of others.

The Centers for Disease Control and Prevention (CDC) defines cognitive development as the learning process of memory, language, thinking, and reasoning. During the first years of life, babies develop bonds of love and trust with their parents and others. This takes place as part of their social and emotional development. The CDC has determined that how babies are cuddled, held, and played with will set the basis for how they interact with their parents (guardians) and others.

I firmly believe that child-care providers are most effective when they use age-appropriate strategies in all areas of early learning. The NAEYC online resource describes developmentally appropriate practice (DAP) as appropriate teaching grounded in research on how children develop and learn in effective early education. This approach, when implemented, will give you confidence in your child's education.

The NAEYC DAP approach involves teachers interacting with children at their age and stage of development. Accomplishing this goal will help each child meet challenges, increase levels of achievement and learning, and increase his or her potential.

Developmentally Appropriate Activities

Teachers and caregivers can consult essential resources and research materials when developing age-appropriate activities. A child's age and stage of development should be considered when planning all activities, which involve providing them with activities at a level that their brains are ready to process. For example, a two- or three-year-old is given an activity—to place the correct color blocks onto a sheet containing the same colors. As the child places the colors onto the sheet, he or she says the name of the color. An infant would not be given this activity.

Child development experts say children should be challenged as their brains mature and are prepared to process new information. An example would be a three- or four-year-old who is taught how to pronounce the names of and recognize the colors and spell and identify items that come in each color during the same activity.

The "Nature, Nurture and Early Brain Development" publication by Sara Gable noted the following information, taken from the book Creative Curriculum for Infants and Toddlers (Dombro et al., 1997), which brought out that caring for infants and toddlers is also about building connections through everyday routines and experiences. During the first three years of life, infants and toddlers look to their caregivers for answers to the following questions: Do people respond to me? Can I depend on other people when I need them? How should I behave? Do people enjoy being with me? What should I be afraid of? Is it safe for me to show how I feel?

Children use emotional expressions to communicate before they learn to talk. Research shows that a baby's positive or negative emotions and the child-care worker's sensitivity to him or her can help support early brain development; for example, a shared positive emotional expression between caregiver and infant, such as smiling and laughing, which positively engages the brain and promotes a feeling of security in the child. Also, when expressions between the child and caregiver are accompanied by heavy emotions, such as sadness and crying, these are remembered and recalled (Dombro et al., 1997).

Continual professional development prepares childcare workers, teachers, and caregivers in this crucial area of child development. Learning how the young brain is stimulated to learn as it grows supports the need for age-appropriate activities, which are fundamental for children's healthy social, emotional, and cognitive growth. As stated earlier, all interactions young children have with adults must be age-appropriate to effectively encourage them as they transition from one level and milestone to the next.

Nurturing the Parent Connection

Like gardeners, parents have different knowledge, skills, and passion levels. A beautiful garden reflects the passion, dedication, and nurturing the gardener is willing to invest. Children reflect the nurturing they receive from adults, especially parents. Parents are an essential factor in nurturing children's cognitive development. The following is an edited excerpt from Missing Link?, a book I penned a few years ago. It contains parents' perspectives on whether or not they felt linked (or connected) to the educational processes of their children.

I started Missing Link? by sharing my experience as a teenage parent, which allowed me to reflect on my involvement in my child's educational process. Through interviews, many parents were willing to share their perspectives as well.

The interviews with parents from Missing Link? are shared to stimulate conversations with parents and encourage collaboration between them and educators. I intend that the reader will better understand how parents feel about their children's educational process and develop ways to connect with and support them.

When I turned eighteen, I became the mother of a beautiful baby girl. I felt prepared to be a mom because I knew how to change and feed a baby's diaper. I was twenty-three when my daughter started kindergarten; I then realized that I did not know how to extend my role as a mom at home to being a parent who supported my child's educational process at her school.

I knew I loved my daughter and wanted the best for her, but I had not received any training or advice on becoming involved in this critical part of her life. I now know I was quietly held accountable even though I did not know what to do.

I came from generations of parents who kept everything to themselves, including how to support their children's education. This may have been because they could not pass on what had not been passed to us. When parents my age talked about their children, it was mostly about how to make them behave. The important thing for us was that our children did not embarrass us in public.

My daughter is now raised with a child of her own, and we have had many discussions about the challenges I faced as a parent during her educational process. As a teacher and school administrator, I had many opportunities to discuss with parents their role in their children's education. Although I did not document those conversations, I knew their importance. The discussions provided significant insight into how their circumstances and challenges in life affected the link they had (or did not have) with their children's education.

After taking an early retirement from school administration, I wanted to continue to dialogue with parents. I feel that it is essential for parents to have an avenue to discuss how they feel and to share their perspectives with other parents and educators—writing Missing Link? provided this avenue.

The parents interviewed in Missing Link? were not parents with whom I had contact as a teacher or school principal. They were parents who accepted an invitation to discuss their perspectives concerning their children's education.

I gained contact with these parents during various life situations, or they were referred to me informally. One-on-one interviews and small group discussions were not conducted methodically. My goal was to serve as an objective observer, not to advance an opinion but to collect feedback.

The parents interviewed were of all age groups and social and economic statuses. Many guardians were parents of school-age children. These guardians might have been relatives who had guardianship of children in school, such as grandparents, uncles, aunts, and siblings who were thrust into the role of parents. In Missing Link? all responsible for raising school-age children were called parents.

When it comes to parents' challenges, parents explain their experiences best. Parents must communicate with each other and those linked to their children's social and academic development. Raising children is a journey that is best not traveled alone. Mistakes can be costly and sometimes irreversible.

What happens in the home has a great deal to do with how a child views the outside world and society.

Research shows that what happens in the home also directly affects how a child responds to his or her environment. For this reason, the parent's viewpoint must be taken seriously. The parent's perspective is valuable when answering the question, "What can educators do to improve student achievement?"

How parents feel about their children's education has to be articulated before we can take the necessary steps to involve them. The responsibility to develop children socially, emotionally, and academically cannot be one-sided, and passing the blame will not solve this dilemma.

Are parents the missing link to their children's social and academic progress? After conducting one-on-one interviews with parents and guardians, I found that parents had strong viewpoints, but some did not know how to articulate their feelings. This may have been because they had never been asked to discuss their perspectives. For this reason, I used limited sometimes edited quotes in Missing Link.

Information concerning parents' perspectives and what they value has to come from them. There cannot be speculation about how parents feel because parents' views sometimes differ from those of the people educating their children. We must meet them where they are in life.

As stated earlier, I decided to write Missing Link? as an avenue for more discussions with parents and to get a deeper understanding and insight into how they felt about the educational process of their children. This was not an attempt to answer questions for the reader; instead, it was an attempt to share parents' perspectives about how their children are being educated and their role in that process.

When I was asked to complete a survey from my child's school, my responses to the survey questions were mainly influenced by what my daughter perceived as a good or bad school experience. All I had to go on were the stories she would share about her day.

The many discussions I had with parents were an attempt to get parents to go beyond what they heard from their children. They were challenged to describe their feelings based on their personal experiences and interactions with the school. As a school administrator, I faced the dilemma of getting parents involved when, in fact, many parents may have felt that they were involved.

The following chapters result from discussions I had with parents on several topics concerning parents' perspectives on their connection to children's education. First, we will discuss the parents' answers to the question, "Do you feel that parents are missing in the educational process of their children?" Next, we will discuss why schools have difficulty getting parents linked to their children's education.

Discussions included empowering parents, who are responsible when a child fails in school, and parents' responsibilities regarding their children's schooling.

Missing Link? provides a better understanding of how parents feel about their role as a link in their children's social, emotional, and academic success. Children's social and academic success chain has many links: parents, school, community, and church. All the links must be present and strong. If there is a weak or missing link, the child's chance for success is in jeopardy.

The following are inserts from my book "The Missing Link?"

Do parents view their involvement in the educational process of their children the same way educators do? If not, does this difference in viewpoint cause educators to perceive parents as missing in the educational process? Parents discussed these observations and many other matters related to the factors that affect how parents view their children's educational process and how their view of these issues affects their children's views.

Other issues found to disconnect or link parents to their children's education are income status, educational level, and generational issues in families.

Parents openly discussed why they feel they are missing in their children's education. One primary reason was that parents may not know what to do or how to help.

A parent of two children in elementary school stated,

"Yes, parents are missing. How can they encourage their children if they do not have an education and the benefits of being educated?"

Some parents do not know the next step besides

attending the Parent-Teacher Organization meetings. They feel it is hard to be a part of their children's educational process if they do not know anything about it. They also feel that parents have not been taught how to support their children's education and have no idea what their role should be at school.

Most moms and dads will try to attend ball games and see their child perform in a play or sing in the school choir. Parents perceived that parents were missing except for these types of activities. They felt that the schools should schedule parent training before or after school plays, ball games, or other activities their children are involved in.

Are children with both the mother and father present in the home at an advantage because the parents can support each other? When asked this question, parents said that this is not always true.

A mother of four said that her husband is missing when it comes to their children's education.

"Because his mother was a single mom, he watched her do everything concerning her kids, and he feels I should also. So I have to take up the responsibility of ensuring one of us stays connected to what is going on with our children's education."

Another parent stated that his mother valued education, but his father did not; he believed in hard work and was street-smart.

"He was not educated but told us that we had to finish high school, and we were afraid not to."

However, when he did finish, his father was not at his graduation. This experience left him with a mixed message from his parents. He revealed that parents must be the ones to push the child. He also shared that one of his children has a learning challenge, so he is laxer with him concerning his school assignments than his daughter, and his daughter became angry with him because he pushed her and not her brother.

He said that maybe he needed to take another look at how he is handling this situation.

"I do not want to send mixed messages about the importance of education to my children like my parents did to my sisters, brothers, and me."

Knowing what is happening in the educational system is challenging for some parents.

As one parent stated,

"Education is always changing, upgrading, or evolving. Keeping up with the educational system seems problematic for many parents. They feel intimidated and do not always discuss this issue with the school."

One area in which they feel school districts have upgraded or evolved is how they communicate with parents. An automated telephone system contacts parents, and the school sends a recorded message to give information about events and school closings. Although the parents said they do not have a problem with this method of communication, some felt that it has diminished the need to have a personal relationship with the school.

A teacher said during the interview that she felt her students' parents were linked with the school because they communicated with her daily by e-mail, the school's website, in the car when they picked up the students, and when they signed off on journals brought home by the students.

Her school provided laptop computers for parents, and the principal did home visits to help the parents set up the computers. She stated that as a parent, she felt that communication was the key and that using technology was one way to do it, and she was okay with it.

A parent who was also an elementary school worker found that parents were uninvolved or missing in their children's education, and she shared the reason she felt this way.

"There is a vicious cycle of parents who are uneducated, and education is not important in the family."

Is it true that low-income parents do not have high expectations for their children's education? One parent explained how she felt in the following remarks:

"I do not believe income determines how parents view their children's education. To generally say that low-income parents do not hold high expectations is untrue. I was raised by a single parent who, at a particular time, was on welfare. Education was a high priority for our family. All of us (my two siblings and I) have college degrees. Two of us have graduate degrees. Low income/poverty does not equal failure. High expectations lead to higher achievement."

A parent with a nine-year-old son in elementary school felt a difference in how low-income and high-income parents viewed their children's education. This parent said,

"Parents with a high income usually are educated or have worked hard to get where they are. Therefore, they pass on to their children the knowledge and experience it takes to be successful. Those parents understand the value of education and that education is an investment. They also position their children to receive the knowledge and experience it will take to succeed.

For example, they put their children in good schools with great programs and activities. In contrast, parents who have low incomes most often depend on federal assistance or work in low-paying jobs. They may not have experienced enough success in their education or the workplace to pass these skills/values to their children. Therefore, they value money more than education because money is tangible and is felt when it is scarce."

The perception of a parent with a high school child is that parents need to invest in their children's education. This parent said,

"You would think low-income parents would care more so that their children would make a better life for themselves and end the generational poverty. However, they do not care as much because they live in survival mode. They are just trying to get their basic needs met. High-income parents know that attaining goals and holding their children to a higher standard is possible. Higher-income parents send their kids to private schools. They are more financially invested in their children's future."

No matter what the circumstances are for the families, parents perceive that it is about holding someone accountable. Parents also shared that in certain aspects, the parents are missing. Nearly all of the parents I spoke with felt that parents with low incomes do not understand the power of influence they have on their children and the educational system.

One teacher and parent of a child in middle school felt that parents should speak up.

"They are often too quiet on important educational issues involving their children. They may relate their income to the value of their vote. They also are not visible in our schools."

Parents also felt that, like low-income parents, parents with high incomes are not very visible because they have time-consuming jobs, but they are not quiet on educational issues and speak out loudly.

They want the best for their children because they feel they contribute significantly through taxes.

One parent had the following perspective:

"I think that all family situations are different. There are parents of low and high-income levels who are not linked to the educational process of their children, and the same can be said for those who are linked. It depends on whether or not they value education."

Does the parent need to be linked with his or her child's school after elementary school? Parents said that their child's elementary school years were more crucial. However, once the child is in middle school, there is more concern about his behavior because he goes through severe hormonal changes, and most children do not have control over their emotions.

One parent imparted the following:

"I do not know if it is less. I think it depends on how much the child is interested in school and whether the child has behavior issues. I have three boys, and they are good kids. I do not have to check on them as much as when they were in elementary school. One of my sons, who is in the tenth grade, has English and reading problems, so I check with his teachers concerning his progress. I also do my part at home with him by having him read and write about what he read, and I check it and make the reading assignment a part of his allowance."

Parents revealed the importance of transitioning children slowly because once they leave the elementary level, changing the amount of pampering and attention would negatively affect them, and they might interpret this to mean that the parents no longer care. Parents sometimes miss elementary school; they feel they do not need to be there the same way. However, some parents felt this was a mistake because even when children are older, they need just as much attention to stay on track—sometimes more.

Parent-teacher communication is even more important because the parent and teacher should work together to solve any issues that prevent the child from succeeding in school, including correcting the child's behavior.

One mother gave the following input:

"As children grow up, we parents teach them to be more independent and start taking responsibility for their schoolwork. My son works hard and tries to stay out of trouble because he knows that if he doesn't, I will be at the school. To boys, it is uncool to have a mom show up at school when you are thirteen as it is when you are five or six."

Another parent felt that fewer learning activities require parents to be engaged at home as the child ages.

"In elementary school, the child needs more help with homework, projects, and other learning activities. As the child gets older, parents perceive less time is needed in this manner. As a parent, communication between the teacher and the parent also declines. My daughter is in the tenth grade. Out of all of her teachers, I only receive communication regarding her progress from two. Even these are not very regular. When I attended the parent/ teacher conference, only one teacher, the dance instructor, gave me tangible ways to help my daughter at home."

A parent of a seventeen-year-old daughter felt that parents are more linked to children's educational process in elementary school because they feel their children still depend on them for security. "In elementary school, they do many milestones, such as their first play and first musical. As children get older, parents tend to loosen their grip and give them more independence. Their education is just as important, but we have established them with the school routine and instilled some basic values, so we no longer have to be at the school once a week."

One educator and parent described how she is on both sides of the fence. "Often, I see myself in the parents' shoes. Parents work so hard to provide their children with the necessities that they rely heavily on the teacher for feedback. Since my job required so much of my time, finding time to visit or check up on my son was hard.

"As an educator, I always encourage parents to visit my class to see what happens and how their children respond to my teaching. I recognized that I had to start eating my own words. My argument was that my son is a good student; however, I realized he valued positive feedback from me, his parent, way more than his teacher. I began to see him responding better to me visiting his class to hang out than coming to talk to his teacher just when he was in trouble or for parent/teacher conferences. My presence in his classroom has made a big difference. My son is not a bad student, but he loves to see me in the class."

In the next chapter, parents share their perspectives concerning being linked to their children's educational process. They discuss what did and did not effectively link them and why.

Getting Parents Linked

Some parents feel they are so caught up with everyday life that they do not have time to engage in their children's education. Low-income parents are concerned with providing their children's basic needs—and even that can be overwhelming.

However, being preoccupied with life situations and circumstances is not only an issue with low-income parents. Many parents felt preoccupied with some aspects of life, such as paying bills, job pressures, and health issues.

Parents also shared that being busy with other children and time restraints kept some of them from being linked to what is going on with each of their children's education. Other parents said that no matter what, parents should make time to be involved in every aspect of their children's lives, and they shared why they feel this is important.

A police officer and parent of fourteen- and seventeen-year-olds stated that he and his wife have always been involved in their children's education through all grade levels. He gave an example of their teamwork when his daughter was accepted into the college of her choice.

He and his wife went to every meeting and college event with her.

He also said,

"We work as a team. My wife and I saw kids being dropped off by their parents and noticed that some parents let them do things independently. It is important for the school and the staff to know that the parents are involved, and the parents should have high expectations for the child and the school."

A father of four children felt that I needed to know a little about his background to fully understand his perspective on his children's education and his role in it. His feelings were tied to how his parents felt about education, and the link was broken when he and his nine siblings were in school. He has tried to repair the damage with his children.

This parent of four shared that his family was poor; his mother had a sixth-grade education, and his father had none. His mother taught his father how to write his name. He could do math in his head, and because he had a photographic memory, people thought he could read. When he was little, his mother would help him read. She would also help him with words he could not pronounce, but as he got older and she had nine children, she did not have time to spend with him. Even though he made straight "A's" in school, his teachers thought he had academic problems. He suspected they did not recognize his academic success because they focused on his family's poor condition. He knew that his family did not have many of the necessities of life. The school fed them with leftover food from the cafeteria. He and his sibling had terrible teeth and few clothes, and because of this, the school staff thought he was an academic special-needs student.

"They thought I could not learn because my family was poor." Because the teachers were young, primarily white teachers, he thought they did not know anything about his culture, and although they tried to help feed his family, they had not been taught how to connect his parents to their children's education.

Parents were unsure what type of training the schools provided for teachers regarding parents, if any, but felt that the parents should be included in the training. The school mainly contacted them when children misbehaved or got hurt. During teacher meetings, the teachers took the lead in the conversation, and the parents were not asked what type of support they needed.

One parent stated, his classwork and homework, or he is not."

Several parents said they felt frustrated when they sometimes could not help with homework because they did not understand it. They were embarrassed to tell the teacher they did not know how to help with school assignments.

Does how parents feel about education affect how their children view education?

A father of a high school student replied,

"That is huge! Parents have to show that they value education by talking to their children about the importance of good grades and going to college. My wife and I always talk to our children about college. We let them know there are no ifs, ands, or buts. They are going to college. We set the bar by being linked to their educational process. We also reward them when they do well with grades and citizenship."

Another parent's perspective:

"If parents feel education is essential, they instill those values in their children. Also, they will be more involved in assisting their child with homework and ensuring he attends school regularly. I think parents must be active in their child's education. Moreover, lead by example."

A fifty-seven-year-old mother of three grown children who is currently in school to complete her high school education stated that she promised her grandchildren that she would get her diploma. She shared the following:

"My parents were uneducated, and of my three children, only one completed high school. I feel that I was affected by my parents' not finishing school, and my not finishing was passed on to my children. I hope my going to back school now will make a difference to my grandchildren."

In the past, she said, she always could get a job. Some years ago, she worked in a factory for ten years and made what she felt was good money. At present, however, she could not get a job. She felt this was not because of her age but because she did not have a high school diploma.

Parents shared that some parents do not realize how vital parent involvement is. They are consumed with their lives and problems and overlook the children's education. Parents also felt there was a lack of resources for the parents.

Does it sound like parents have many explanations for why they are not involved in their children's education? When asked for any good reasons not to know what was happening with their children, all the parents I spoke to said no. They realized that parents needed to find a way to balance things out.

Parents admit that they need help. For example, schools could offer classes for parents, such as budgeting finances and time management. They acknowledged that some parents need to learn parenting skills and that parenting skills consist of more than learning about academics and how to read test scores.

One parent said that she was frustrated.

"When the state test ISTEP is given at my child's school, they schedule a time to discuss the results with parents. I understand the importance of ISTEP but feel that I cannot do anything to help after the fact."

As stated earlier, the parents' frame of mind and focus is reflected in their children. The children bring whatever their parents are going through at home to school daily.

A state police officer and parent of two school-aged children stated,

"Parents who set higher educational standards for their children usually have high-achieving students who have education as a top priority. Parent satisfaction with the school also affects children's feelings about education. If a parent is delighted, it will manifest positively in the child's performance and behavior."

To create effective parent and school connections, one parent felt a need to feel welcome when they visit the school. "The schools should make the parents feel that they care about them and what they go through and give them the support they need." Parents perceived that being made to feel welcome in the school would replace the occasional feeling of being blamed and not understood. One parent stated that when she spoke to the school about her child's failing grades, she felt they could not care less about her, and she began to shut down and feel helpless and overpowered in the situation.

Another parent who felt very welcome at her children's school stated,

"The principal and teachers are good at keeping me

informed. They return my phone calls, and when I visit the school, they call me by name and know my child's name." Being linked with their children's education was also important to parents because they felt this meant knowing their child's teacher, school policies and politics, and volunteering to meet other parents.

According to a parent of a college student, parents should make themselves known in their child's school.

"You know you are linked when important people in the school (e.g., principal, teachers, and counselors) can put your face with your name. This happens when you participate in activities like visiting the classroom, helping with homework, and attending parent/teacher conferences."

Other activities parents mentioned included reading to their children's class and being part of parent groups. Parents also believe that being linked means that parents need to know who their children are and what they are involved in. This means taking the time to listen and learn about their interests. Sometimes, it means pushing the issue until communication happens.

Parents confirmed that they should help children succeed in getting an education, and when they are involved, their children appreciate and know that they care about them.

Most importantly, it lets their children know that the parents support their education, sports events, or whatever they do.

One parent said concerning this,

"If we, as parents, do not care, our children will be affected by our attitude and develop a negative attitude toward school and sometimes even life. It is up to the home to keep children motivated. In the school setting, parent involvement should be that of the observer. The school system should be set up to educate the child thoroughly, and reinforcement should happen at home."

Parents must realize that the link with their children's education also affects their social and emotional well-being. Parents felt this is important because it directly relates to children's success in all areas of their lives. They also believed that for some parents, education was not a priority for various reasons. Therefore, their participation in their children's education is lacking.

For single parents, this may be because they work and cannot attend parent-teacher meetings or other activities usually scheduled during the school day or before they get off work. As stated earlier, some parents, single or otherwise, are not aware of how best to be involved and support education at home.

One single dad emphasized the importance of his role as his two-year-old daughter's first teacher. He feels he sets the example of what she can expect from life.

"I am her protector and will be involved from the beginning with her education. She will be aware of my presence, even when I am not there, because she knows I may come to the school anytime. Some students are not focused, so they are lost. It is the parents' responsibility to help their children stay focused."

This sense of responsibility and motivation is vital to effective parental involvement.

Another single parent preparing his son for preschool felt that parents need to monitor what their children are being taught.

"Ever since he was six months old, I have said his ABCs with him daily. I know some toys will do this, but I feel it is important for me to do it. My parents read to us, and Mom did not allow anyone to use baby talk when talking to her children. I feel that parents need to make the time needed to monitor what their children are being taught and spend productive time with them."

As shared through the parents' perspectives, being linked to children's education through knowledge and communication is a powerful tool. The discussions in the following chapter will attest to what parents feel would empower them and why they need to be empowered concerning their children's education, reinforcing their capability to make a difference.

Empowering Parents

Educators across America and the world have researched how to improve parental involvement for decades. The answer has been consistently linked to student academic success, discipline, and attendance issues, underscoring parents' crucial role in their children's education.

I asked parents what they could do to empower themselves to be positive links in their children's educational process. Many parents felt they should ask themselves, "If we do not get involved with our children, why should we expect the schools to take up our issues?"

The following discussion began with an explanation of being empowered as a parent. Empowerment means more than being involved with school programs, such as athletics. It means that parents know how to effect the necessary changes and demands to influence their children's educational process and ensure that effective academic and social developmental strategies are implemented in the school.

One of the things parents felt was necessary was

that schools should have more conversations with parents about how they feel about their children's education and empower parents to educate and evaluate their children. Steps should be taken to bridge the communication gap by understanding what type of learning experiences children are reaching. It may seem that some parents do not care because they do not come to the school or call frequently.

Many of the parents I spoke with felt communication was one way they could be empowered. All forms of communication, such as calls, letters, e-mails, and the Internet, would be helpful. Effective, consistent, and informative communication is the key.

A parent who felt that parents should not be surprised when a child brings home a bad report card also stated,

"There should be communication with the parent at the first sign of failure so that the problem can be identified and corrected, whether it is a home or school issue."

Another parent shared that communication is assertive.

"I think the schools just need to communicate with the parents constantly. I like the web grades, where you can check your child's progress anytime. I like the automated calls I receive when my child misses class. I also think that in high school, the school counselor should meet with the parents and a student to discuss the student's educational progress; this type of communication is powerful."

Parents believe that they should be educated on the positive results of their involvement. Parents have different means, abilities, and needs; the school can create classes for parents based on this information. The school should also have strict rules for students and parents. Parents agree that there should be consequences for students who break the rules and for parents.

They felt that some parents might have to break the generational habits of their parents and grandparents, who were not involved in their children's education, and that maybe the church could also be the link for spiritual guidance and support.

One grandmother who is the guardian of her daughter's school-age children said,

"If there are no past role models for parents in their family, they do not know what it is to be empowered to support their children's education. They have not had an example of how to communicate effectively with the school, and this can be intimidating and cause the link to be broken or never happen."

I invited a twenty-year-old guardian to discuss her perspectives with me. This young adult has taken over the guardianship of her sister's teenage daughter. She now has the legal responsibility of a parent for her niece's health, security, and education. During our discussion concerning empowering parents, she shared that her niece's school does not take her wanting to be involved in her educational process seriously.

There was a lack of communication from the teachers, but it soon improved when she regularly showed up at the school. She also shared the following,

"When you are having a grown-up life while people see others your age partying, it is hard for them to take your role as a concerned parent to a teenager seriously. I know I am a parent, and I need to have the same power as other parents because I influence my niece's dreams and visions as they do for their children. I have high expectations for my niece."

This guardian said there was a problem when she discovered that her expectations of educational issues differed from those of her niece's biological mother and her family. She felt that when one becomes the guardian of an older child and does not know that child's history, one may be unprepared to make the necessary decisions concerning her education and other issues.

She added,

"My niece had been told that she was doing well in school. I found that 'doing well' to her mother and other members of my family was a 2.0 GPA and issues with fighting the other students when things did not go her way. I need to be empowered by the school, but my family has asked me if I will turn this young lady around. No one sat down with me and wanted to know what I was going through. No one knows your sacrifice with a child; they only see the product."

One parent compared parents of the fifties, sixties, and seventies to modern parents. He felt that today's parents are disconnected. He also felt that the disconnection may have happened because "the neighborhoods have changed," and the black family he knew had changed.

"We have turned away from being a spiritual group of people and have allowed the media to dictate how we bring up our children. During my parents' day, there were partnerships with families and schools. The school knew that the family would discipline and do their part, but today's modern-day parents expect the school to be both parent and instructor, and they do not see anything wrong with it. Black educated people moving out of their neighborhoods could also be a cause because the children do not see examples of all the different professions that people who look like them and come from the same place are involved in."

A parent of three children in school, one at each grade level—elementary, middle, and high school students—felt that parents are empowered by getting to know their children's teachers, counselors, and coaches.

They should read the information the school sends home and ask questions about the school and their children. She also shared that parents cannot be lazy regarding the hard work it takes to ensure their children are getting the proper education. She concluded,

"If parents teach their children to respect authority, work hard, and value education, they will model that.

Children will also model that if a parent is lazy and apathetic."

When asked about how they, as parents, could be empowered, two parents' perspectives were as follows:

"The more I know about my son's teachers and how they operate their classrooms, the more I am empowered. I like to know his/her teaching methods, his/her expectations for my child, and how my son responds to him/her. I learn these things by visiting the classroom, communicating often with his teachers, and communicating with my son. I would also like to know about the school's performance as a whole, what programs they offer, and the diversity of the staff. Knowledge is power, so the more I know about the teacher, the school, and the school district, the more it empowers me to be involved in my son's education. Parents have more power of influence than they know."

The other parent felt that whether they value education or not, the lack of involvement will hurt their children, but they have a positive effect when they are involved. They teach their children principles such as diligence, a good work ethic, effort, consistency, and that education is worth more than fast cash. They do this by ensuring their children are on top of things, such as turning in assignments on time and completing homework. They read material, have children read to them, and make learning fun. She said,

"When parents do not get involved, children do not receive those important principles, and the effects spill over into adulthood. Those children often have difficulty holding jobs and paying bills on time and usually depend on federal assistance."

A father of five children—two grown, two in college, and one on the way to college—felt that a parent has to want to be empowered.

"The empowerment comes from whatever the parents' desires are; if the parents want to be involved, they will attend meetings, activities, and school events. In other words, parents empower themselves.

When they step away, they give all the decisions about their child to the school, which may or may not be good."

Parents perceived that it was powerful to show up and be seen at the school, so the school knew they were caring parents. The parent shared,

"The schools need to know that they want to be a

part of the educational process in a positive way and are not there to call the teacher a liar and cuss administration. I feel that parents should go to the school to be supportive. Parents are empowered by being there."

Parents gave many reasons for not being there for their children. However, they agreed that all stakeholders are responsible when a child fails. Most parents agree they have the utmost responsibility for their children's success. The next chapter will give insight into this meaningful discussion.

Responsibilities

Whose fault is it when a child fails in school? Parents feel that the school, community, home, church—all the stakeholders—and the child each play a role in the child's success and must be held accountable when he fails. During our discussions, parents believed they needed to be responsible for their children's education. Three of the parents' perspectives concerning this issue are as follows:

"Teachers educate, but it is on the parents to ensure the education is effective for their children."

"Discipline at home is important because if the parents cannot control the child at home and make him do his homework, then what chance does the school have in the classroom?"

"Whatever the parents' value, the children will value because parents are the only example some of them see. I am an educator, so I lead by example so that my children will value education. They were not given a choice as to whether or not they were going to college. ... I told them, 'You may not want to go to college, but you are going from here.' I am responsible for enforcing their value and not letting them drift through life."

When it pertains to children, responsibility comes in many forms. One parent felt that the words were discouraging and that negative words spoken to a child can have a devastating effect. She felt that when teachers prejudge a child's social and economic environment, this judgment can lead to a student's failing attitude.

This parent shared a situation involving a high school counselor who told a student who wanted to be a doctor that she could not be because there were no doctors in her family. She felt this remark discouraged the young lady and was responsible for the student's decision to drop out of school. She stated,

"Everyone who connects with the student should feel some responsibility for her success. Words are powerful."

Another parent said,

"In a broad sense, there is often a correlation between the level of education and income. I think it is hard to break when it is a generational thing, such as generational poverty. However, no matter your economic situation, the family is still responsible for the success or failure of its children. They will need more support, but they are also responsible for seeking out the support they need."

Meeting the needs of her three children is a challenge for one parent. This parent expressed her need by saying,

"It would be beneficial for teachers to provide parents with information on how they can engage in learning activities with their child in the home, using everyday situations. They can communicate this through e-mail, newsletters, etc. Parents should also initiate these discussions with their teachers.

Perhaps a return to discussions on how parents can best be involved in their children's education is in order. Parents must continue to inquire about their children's school day, review their homework, look at their assignments and textbooks, and use teachable moments to relate everyday life to what their children are learning in school."

A parent of a child diagnosed with attention deficit hyperactive disorder (ADHD) commented that she asked her son's school for help with her child because she did not know what to do or how to handle a child with ADHD. The school was not able to provide her with assistance. She feels that schools should be responsible for providing a variety of parenting classes and family involvement activities. She felt that the parent's interaction with the child at home is linked with how the child responds to adults and his peers at school, so it would be helpful for the school and home to modify a child's behavior consistently.

She also stated that.

"Maybe parents would have a more productive link with the schools if they felt that they were working together for the good of the whole child."

Parents understood the home was responsible for ensuring children had school materials such as pencils and notebooks.

Another parent said,

"Parents should give their children more than school supplies; parents should also supply children with emotional support. When a parent is emotionally missing in their children's education, their children feel lost. They do not care about their schoolwork because they feel no one at home cares. You cannot teach a child who does not desire to learn; that should be reinforced at home."

Do parents realize how vital this emotional link is

with their children's educational process? Do they need support and training in a child's basic daily needs?

Schools may take for granted that parents ensure children get enough rest at night and are well-fed. Parents feel they should be doing such things and keeping children safe by knowing where they are and monitoring their friends, but this does not always happen. Child experts have suspected that a child's academic failures are often symptoms of other problems.

One parent summed it up by commenting,

"Academic success starts at home and flows with them through school. If parents set the standards from day one, the student will know the expectations. When a student fails, the parents, principal, and teacher must look closely to see why this happened and what can be done to get the child on the right track or in the right school."

Another observation was that parents who are not involved with their children's education—for example, parents who miss parent-teacher conferences multiple times without a valid reason—should be charged fees. The money should be given to the school to help with programs.

The parent who made this observation commented,

"If all stakeholders were involved, it would allow for all thoughts, ideas, suggestions, possible problems, and solutions to be utilized in bringing up a successful child. Everyone who has contact with a child shares in the responsibility. If the child fails, we have all had a hand in the failure. Parents, especially, should know if their child is successful at school, and if the child is not learning, they should do whatever is needed to improve their learning situation at home and school. Parents should never stop being held responsible for their children's educational progress."

A high school principal and parent shared that he has witnessed parents giving up responsibility for their high school children. They start to decrease responsibility in middle school, he said. In contrast, during the elementary years, they feel that "this is my baby," so they sometimes hold themselves more responsible than they hold the school. His perspective was,

"Whether or not parents feel responsible has a lot to do with parents feeling that children are more independent in high school. They may feel this way because they are tired of the challenges of having adolescent children. I have found that when a male child reaches ten to twelve years of age, single mothers feel that they need more help controlling him and will hold the school more responsible for the academic and social behavior of the child."

Another parent said that she felt responsible for her child not finishing high school because she did not finish. She is fifty-seven years old and is currently enrolled in an adult high school, attempting to earn a diploma. She is one of six girls raised by a single mom. She shared that her mother did not push education on her children. She was okay as long as they made a passing grade of a "D."

She also shared that her mother wanted them out of school; she did not care if they finished high school because she knew she could not send them to college.

"My mother felt her responsibility was to feed the family; she did this by working two jobs. She did not get her high school diploma but did a good job raising us without an education. We never went to jail or did drugs. She taught us morals, values, and ethics. We were taught to talk to adults, treat people, and be polite.

The mothers in the neighborhood felt that it was their responsibility to educate the girls by teaching them how to set the table, sew, and knit. My family let the children make their own decisions about education. I hold myself responsible for getting pregnant and quitting school in the tenth grade."

This parent also shared that she had three children. One of her children did not finish high school, and he stayed in trouble. She said it was hard to encourage him to finish school because he knew she did not.

"When I decided to return to school to get my diploma, my son returned, and I am so proud of him. We both are at home, trying to do homework and asking each other questions. Sometimes, my other children, his brother and sister, help us.

Returning to school has positively affected my children, just like quitting school hurt them. I would also like to think that my example of going back to school at my age is responsible for encouraging my son to value education now while he is still young."

Another perspective of parents was that parents sometimes hold the child's friends responsible. They find ways to blame their child's bad social behavior on his friends.

One father of a teenager said that he has heard parents say,

"'If he were not hanging with that bad boy in his school, he would not do the things he does.' The truth is that it is the responsibility of the parents to train their child how to choose the right friends. This is a part of his social development."

The parent of a four-year-old girl who will start school the following year felt a huge disconnection between the family and the school, and this may be because the family unit does not seem to be an essential part of society anymore.

He said,

"Some parents see the school as a daycare and a way to get their children out of their hair. Kids are on their own to try to figure out and navigate their way through the education system and sometimes even life."

Another parent's viewpoint concerning being responsible was, "For the most part, if parents are missing out on their kid's education, the parent is to blame. Schools give parents many opportunities to play an active role; parents too often do not prioritize it.

It is a shared responsibility between parents, the school, and the community. The school has a job, but parents should be their backup; that means turning off the television and cell phones and working with the child. It also takes the whole community supporting the success of the child."

It was interesting to discuss their children's education with them. As I spoke with them, I began to categorize their comments. I then used the different categories to create a summary of our discussions.

Summing Up the Discussion

Missing Link? was concluded by summarizing my discussions with parents. I hope this type of open dialogue with parents will not end. I felt that it was important that parents were not restricted or influenced in the way they responded during our conversations.

I desired to gain parents' perspectives on their children's educational process, emphasizing their role. By doing so, child-care providers would better understand how to connect with parents. Many questions developed from the conversations. Getting parents to share how they felt by discussing emerging questions proved a valuable way for them to communicate their perspectives. Common responses to the questions were put into categories; the categories were used to make summations about the conversations.

As a result, parents of different social and economic statuses have shared and can continue to learn from each other's experiences. Summarizing the overall perspectives that parents shared can yield several conclusions.

From the discussions, we find that parents need

to be empowered and informed to do so. They must be included and play an active, influential role in their children's education. This may mean providing resources and the support parents need, such as time management and parenting classes, which will ensure that parents are equipped with the necessary tools.

As active participants in their children's education, parents need to be present at school to ensure that all children receive the support they need to succeed academically and socially. The key to this is open and effective communication.

Parents also expressed the need to create a positive school experience. They understand that when all stakeholders are united, a strong support system is formed for the child. The community, home, church, and school should form a supportive network to help children overcome challenges and avoid failure. Each link in this network is crucial for success.

Weak links also need to be identified and strengthened. Another perspective was to hold themselves more accountable. Parents cannot let life challenges and their endeavors keep them from knowing what is happening with their children. They realized they could not always wait for schools to offer them the needed support system. Most parents determined that they would have to seek and request support.

Another factor concerning how parent influence their children was shared. It was identified that how parents perceive ideals— "We are what we think"; "We accomplish what we know we can"; "Education is important and should be given priority"; and many more personal beliefs—that motivate how their children feel and may set the groundwork for their success and failure in school.

Parents strongly expressed that schoolteachers and administrators should not assume that parents do not care about their children's education because they are low-income. Support systems and conversations need to happen for parents of all ethnic and socioeconomic stations in life.

As I spoke with parents of different cultural and economic backgrounds, they all expressed that, at times, life challenges prevent them from giving their children's education their full attention. Parents of higher economic status are sometimes more invested in their children's education and, therefore, are more involved with monitoring their investment by ensuring their children are being educated in the best possible way.

Parents who are less invested and overwhelmed with everyday survival felt that if their children are fed and have clothes to wear to school, the school should appreciate their efforts. If the children do not perform well in school, it is up to the teachers and the school to support them.

Until educators genuinely communicate and understand parents' perspectives, they will continue to determine that parents are the missing link—but are they?

Most of the parents I spoke with felt they were missing something in their children's educational process. Some parents were satisfied with their roles but thought that because they defined their roles differently from the school system, the school did not feel they were doing enough. The parents deemed that they were doing all that they could.

A few parents blamed themselves for not being linked to or caring enough to be linked to their children's education. They felt they had enough to worry about getting through day-to-day concerns and survival.

"I no longer have a ... us-against-them mentality," said one parent, "and I see the importance of all the links in supporting our children's education. We all pay the price when one link is weak or missing because if children are unsuccessful, they will burden their parents and society."

Parents also shared that having the discussions helped them reflect on their involvement in their children's education and the importance of staying connected with their overall academic and social development.

After our discussions, the parents expressed gratitude for the chance to talk openly about their feelings. Some of them revealed that the discussions helped them reevaluate whether or not they were linked to their children's educational process.

I want parents to know that it is okay to ask questions and have conversations with other parents and those educating their children. Listening to parents' perspectives can teach us much. The interview questions were designed to encourage and motivate conversations with parents.

The responses to the questions became the discussion topics for the chapters of the book Missing Link. No methodical circumstances were used; however, I created a method to share parent responses organized and accurately for the reader.

Parent quotes were not transcribed. I took notes, redirected questions, and used open-ended questioning to glean parent perspectives.

It was interesting to discuss their children's education with them. Many studies show that parents who stay connected to the educational process help nurture their children's cognitive development. Children with involved parents are motivated to achieve.

Nurturing the Whole Child

An article by Kim Austin, an American Rose Society (ARS) consulting rosarian, quoted an English poet Alfred Austin, who wrote, "The glory of gardening: hands in the dirt, head in the sun, heart with nature, to nurture a garden is to feed not just the body, but the soul." She felt that this poem caused her to ponder, "Why do I grow roses? Why do I garden when it requires blood, sweat, and tears?"

Mind

Like the rosarian Kim Austin, caring for children may cause caregivers to wonder if caring for someone else's children is worthwhile. Fortunately, many fight through this and continue to put their passion for children at the forefront. Today, most children spend Monday through Friday in a child-care facility as parents work to provide for them.

My experience supporting and training child-care workers and parents has caused me to admire their passion, dedication, and sacrifice. I feel that they are sometimes on what I call the battlefield for children—on the battlefield, fighting for children's social, emotional, and academic success. As a society, we have fought for many things— the right to bear arms, free speech, and the freedom to choose. I am talking, however, about fighting for the rights of children who must be healthy and whole.

Children have the right to be nurtured and given everything they need to succeed. When children are unmanageable, confused, and unmotivated, somehow, we blame them. Children need a weapon against things that can defeat them. The most potent weapons in this battle are the adults in their lives, most notably the caregivers and parents. Parent refers to anyone legally responsible for the child (e.g., grandparent, aunt, or guardian). Of course, children need other weapons and strategies, such as community, church, and government, to be on the battlefield.

Usually, when we hear the phrase "mind, body, and spirit," it describes the being of an adult. However, it is essential to remember that children are little human beings. Nurturing the whole child considers his or her mind, body, and spirit; this embraces the child's social, emotional, and cognitive health.

Like flowers in a garden, children flourish outdoors. Children love to be out in the sun, fresh air, wind, and rain. If they could, they would take off all of their clothes and dance, jump, and run around naked, eating dirt. They would be happy to play in the mud and splash in puddles. This activity supports the child's free will.

Merriam-Webster defines the mind as "the intellectual or rational faculty in man, the understanding; the intellect; the power that conceives, judges, or reasons; and the entire nature; the soul often distinguishes from all the body. The state at any given time of the faculties of thinking, willing, choosing, and like, psychical activity or state, choice, inclination, liking, intent and will."

Mental health experts state that the mind of a child with good mental health will think clearly, develop socially and cognitively, and build self-esteem and self-regulation.

When we look at a flower garden, the beauty of the flowers reveals that experts take care of it. The mental well-being of children is not always as obvious. Caregivers must look to the experts to ensure a child's mind is developing correctly.

According to mental health experts, a child's caregivers should be just as diligent in helping to prevent mental health issues as they are in preventing physical illnesses and injuries. Mental health needs must be identified at an early age. The website Mental Health America: Children's Mental Health Matters suggests the following basic needs to ensure good mental health: 1.) Give unconditional love and nurture a child's confidence and self-esteem, 2.) Encourage children to play; 3.) Enroll children in an after-school activity; 4.) Provide a safe and secure environment; 5.) Give appropriate guidance and discipline when necessary, 6.) Communicate and get help if there is a concern about a child's mental health.

For more information on identifying mental health issues in children and what parents and teachers can do, go to the Mental Health America website at www. mentalhealthamerica.net.

Body

Webster's Dictionary defines a person as "a human being frequently in composition; as anybody, nobody, and somebody. As distinguished from the spirit, or vital principle; the physical person." A child's body goes through many transitional stages on the journey to adulthood. It is no accident that child-care facilities and schools provide nutritionally balanced meals for children. As a school principal, I monitored what was being served to the children in the cafeteria.

I had to meet with the nutritionist to discuss the children's complaint that the cafeteria did not offer enough variety. During the conversation, I learned why certain items were offered and not others (possible allergies, for example) and that the meals were balanced to ensure the nutritional needs of all children were met (it is the law).

Plants need nourishment to grow to their full potential, beauty, and reproduction ability. Proper nourishment is vital to the growth and well-being of children as well. What happens when flowers do not get enough water, or the soil lacks nutrients? The leaves can wither, and blooms will fall off; the flowers are not as beautiful and can even die. The effect of malnutrition on children has been well documented. When a woman is pregnant, she must receive the proper nourishment for herself and the child.

Spirit

The mother's nutrition during pregnancy is crucial to the child's health. If the mother is malnourished, then the child she is carrying will be malnourished—Moreover, this can have devastating and lasting effects on the child.

Studies show that malnourishment can impede social, emotional, and cognitive development and affect the reproductive and productive health of the child into school-age and adulthood. An article by Sagan and Druyan (1994) reveals that if children are not well nourished during their first years, their ill health will affect their ability to learn, think, and communicate. The article also stated that when the body does not get enough food, it must decide how to invest in the limited nourishment available. Survival will come first, growth is second, and learning will last. This underscores the long-term consequences of malnutrition on a child's future health and development.

Just as plants can be overwatered, children can overeat. Experts define malnutrition as a condition that results from eating a diet that does not have enough or has too many nutrients. Not enough nutrients is called "undernutrition"; too much is called "overnutrition." If undernutrition occurs during pregnancy or before age two, the lack of proper nurturance could cause permanent underdeveloped physical and mental development; a balanced nutritional foundation is needed to nurture the child's body to its full potential.

I have included the sections on mind, body, and spirit to encourage readers of Nurture to see children as little human beings who are solely dependent on the adults in their lives as they develop into the people they will become. These little human beings must learn how to manage the different aspects of life. They inevitably understand moral and ethical behavior.

Children who learn to pray begin to learn about having a relationship with God. Punishment should not be the premise behind why they strive to be decent people. Children should be taught how to connect with their emotional selves through having a good spirit. The most heartbreaking vision is a child with a sad or broken spirit.

I shared earlier that children think about suicide at young ages. As adults, we should be morally responsible for children's spiritual well-being. The relationships that children have with adults can strengthen or break their spirits. You may recall that children are molded by the relationships they have with the adults in their lives. For this reason, children's caregivers should resist viewing children as little things that should be played with and then set aside when the caregivers are too tired or do not want to be bothered. They should know that children are our first and most important priority.

Merriam-Webster defines a person's spirit as the rational and immortal part of humans—that part of humans that enables them to think and the emotional part of human nature. It is the seat of feeling distinct from intellect, the vehicle of individual personal existence, the surviving entity. A broken spirit is hard to mend. As a child, I experienced having a broken Spirit.

When My Spirit Was Broken

I was a timid child, living with eight siblings and my parents. I always wanted to make my mother proud of me early on. I wanted to grow up to be someone who would make a difference in the world. When I started school, I remember being very upset when my mother left me there with people I did not know.

My next memory of school is when I was in the fourth grade. I strongly desired to be in Ms. Smith's fifth-grade class. I did all my work in the fourth grade, even homework. The teacher seemed pleased with me until the last day of school, when she told me I would not be passed to the fifth grade and would have to repeat the fourth.

I cried and begged her to let me pass. I cried so long and hard that she finally said she would pass me if I went to summer school and received As and Bs. She also gave me her phone number. I stopped crying and went home, but my heart was still broken because I had to face my family.

That summer, I went to school and worked very hard. Throughout the summer I called my fourth-grade teacher, wanting to tell her how hard I was working and that. I was making good grades. However, Whenever I called her, the person who answered the phone said she was in Florida. I remember doing nothing else that summer except schoolwork and calling my teacher. As a result of my hard work, I earned all "A's" and one "B."

At the start of the new school year, I was excited to

show her my report card so that I could be promoted to Ms. Smith's fifth-grade class. On the first day of school, I greeted my fourth-grade teacher with a big smile and handed her my report card; I waited for her response. She looked at me and said. "This is good, but you cannot attend Ms. Smith's class. You are still in the fourth grade." She then reached into her desk and handed me a souvenir soap dish from Florida, saying, "This is for you."

After that, I experienced a heavy feeling that I cannot explain. My spirit was broken, and I did not care about school anymore. This is part of my passion for ensuring that all children receive the nurturing they need. I carried this heaviness to high school. In my senior year, I became pregnant and gave birth to a little girl.

As I held my daughter in my arms, I realized that my life had changed—now, I was responsible for another life. As I watched her grow from an infant to a toddler, I realized that this little person needed more from me than food and clothing. I would need to keep her safe as she explored the world around her.

No one told me how to do that as my daughter went through each stage—walking, talking, and entering school.

I did not know to put her in preschool, so her first day of school was kindergarten. I did not want to leave her there; her first day was more challenging for me than it was for her. I felt I had no control over what would happen to her throughout the day. She was becoming a part of the world that would influence her social and emotional development.

I was unsure what social and emotional development meant or how to protect her from any damage she could obtain from interacting with adults and peers. It seemed that my daughter became a teenager overnight, and I knew she would leave for college soon. I always wanted to give her something she could take with her—my faith. She had my love, and I wanted her to know that no matter what happened to her in life, she could always look to God to keep her spirit strong.

Children's souls are nurtured and cared for When exposed to love, security, and faith. A cared-for soul is happy, and a happy child's soul can conceive of who he or she is, be resilient, and find his or her place in this world.

Creating Nurturing Environments

During a visit to a local garden nursery, I observed an environment conducive to healthy plant growth. The caregivers were trained, and they seemed to have a passion for what they were doing. The plants were nurtured in a way that was different for each variety. In the same way, when one enters a preschool, the environment should demonstrate that children are socially, emotionally, and cognitively nurtured.

A nurturing home is equally important. According to the National Center for Children in Poverty, negative early experiences, such as poverty, can impair children's mental health and affect cognitive, social, and emotional development. However, with the potential of child-care facilities to provide nurturing environments, there is inspiration and motivation to create such environments for children's developmental health.

According to "America's Children in Brief: Key National Indicators of Well-Being, 2015" revealed that in 2011, 49 percent of children ages birth to four years old with employed mothers were primarily cared for by a relative; 24 percent spent most of their time in a child-care facility; and 13 percent were cared for by a non-relative in a home environment, such as with a nanny or babysitter.

Among children in families in poverty in 2011, 18 percent were in child-care facilities, and 19 percent were with a relative who was not their mother, father, or grandparent. By comparison, a more significant percentage of children in families at or above the poverty level were in child-care facilities (26 percent), and only 4 percent were cared for by other relatives. In 2012, about 62 percent of children ages three to six and not in kindergarten were in child-care facilities.

However, many studies show no conclusive evidence that child-care facilities, on average, are either better or worse for the development of children than for them being cared for by parents.

Research shows that nurturing and supportive care consistently and developmentally soundly positively affects children and their parents. Most importantly, high-quality childcare, emphasizing healthy social, emotional, and cognitive development, provides parents with a reassuring and confident choice. To learn more about quality early learning education and childcare, visit naeyc.org.

Low-income children who attend intensive, nurturing, high-quality early education programs have tremendous school success, higher graduation rates, lower levels of juvenile crime, decreased need for special education services, and lower teenage pregnancy rates than their peers (F. et al., 2000).

As allotted earlier, The National Center for Injury Prevention and Control (CDC) document stated that because children experience their world through the relationships and interactions they have with adults, these relationships must be safe, stable, and nurturing. These three qualities also apply to the environment to which children are exposed daily because they make a difference for children as they grow and develop.

An article by Linda Dusenbury, PhD, on the Education World website shared that children need to feel safe to learn. "One of the most important things teachers can do to promote learning is to create classroom environments where students feel safe."

Communication, collaboration, and personal sacrifice for children's good will be necessary to create nurturing preschool environments.

Working Together to Creating a Nurturing Environment for Children

Every adult—teachers (and co-teachers), classroom assistants, lead teachers, directors (supervisors, administration), and parents—must be committed to creating a nurturing preschool environment. My observations of the interaction between teachers and the administration revealed that they must work together to make this a reality. A nurturing environment for children cannot be burdened with adult conflict. A nurturing environment for children cannot result in bad attitudes between adults.

There is an old saying, "It takes a village to raise a child," yet most people say the village no longer exists. Who are we talking about when we say "village" today? The village is different from past interpretations. Today, the adults in the child-care facilities are a large part of the village. This means all must focus on the needs of children because child-care workers are a part of raising someone else's children.

Children watch, learn, and model what they see adults doing. Adult interactions must be consistent with the social and emotional lessons the children in their care are expected to master. The adults' relationship is a part of the children's reality. The children see how the adults interact and hear what the adults say about each other.

Communication

When children do not see the correct modeling of behavior and witness outbursts and quarreling among the adults, feelings of insecurity and distrust can develop. Child-care experts have long suggested that for children to thrive, they must feel secure and safe.

Co-teachers can have a wonderful experience when planning and communication are in place. This can be done by establishing rapport with each other. During my many visits to child-care facilities, I have witnessed what happens when co-teachers do not communicate. There is an uncomfortable relationship between them and the children, who, in turn, feel uncomfortable. The daily activities do not flow, which causes escalated discipline issues.

Planning can create a positive relationship between co-teachers. This means communicating to minimize misunderstandings, determining each other's teaching and classroom-management styles, and using them to create a cohesive, stable classroom. Knowing each other's strengths and weaknesses can help develop a positive rapport and resolve problems before they escalate. The key is to discuss and plan to avoid getting into a heated discussion in front of the children.

Collaboration

When the adults collaborate, they can use their styles to complement each other, creating a nurturing environment for children. Child-care teachers and directors should have consistent expectations and be on the same page about instruction, discipline, and parent communication. Decisions for the facility should involve collaboration with all, not done in isolation. Suggestions for collaborating with parents include the following: Involve parents in the development of the school's discipline policy, offer parent-support workshops (e.g., on discipline and parenting), and create parent groups like the PTO in elementary schools.

I observed one interaction between the supervisors

and administrators of a child-care facility that caused me concern. They made a significant decision about the children's rotation—changing the time teachers spent with each age group—without involving the teachers. When this change was implemented, it was evident that there was no commitment from the teachers, who felt that the decision prevented them from bonding with the children and their parents.

In this case, the administration took my suggestion to bring the issue back to the table and invite teacher input. The result was a collaborative plan with everyone committed to the children's good.

Personal Sacrifice

Nurturing children is one of the world's most essential and unrecognized jobs. Creating a nurturing environment requires personal sacrifice, which means putting the needs of the children first by being willing to overlook the imperfections of others and working together as a team. It also means being willing to recognize personal weaknesses and sacrifice time for training to increase the skills needed to nurture children.

Personal sacrifice also means that the caregiver puts aside adverse reactions to what is happening in his or her personal life and maintains a positive attitude and demeanor for the children. This does not mean being a pretender but doing whatever is necessary to sincerely prevent social or emotional damage to the children with whom the caregiver interacts. Your sacrifice is not in vain; it profoundly and positively impacts the children you care for.

Caregivers should realize that they are not just individuals but an essential part of a team. Without everyone's dedication, creating a nurturing environment for children is impossible. Your role is crucial, and your efforts are valued. This recognition of your value should motivate you to continue your efforts.

Conclusion

My passion for preventing developmental damage to young children moved me to pen Nurture. Personal observations in child-care facilities revealed that child-care workers, such as preschool teachers, understand the need for age-appropriate activities and learning strategies. However, connecting cognitive development with the social and emotional development of young children was unintentionally overlooked and misunderstood by most. This connection is crucial when young children transition through each stage of their development. Research shows that young children who are socially and emotionally stable learn, thrive, and grow up to have a more positive teenage experience.

Children's differences come from genetics and situations they are exposed to, socially, emotionally, and cognitively. As they grow and develop, whatever they are exposed to becomes the ground that nurtures or depletes them. Child-care professionals should obtain expertise in all areas of child development. Children are not only our product but the future of this world.

Just as gardeners seek the expertise of rosarians to obtain the skills necessary to grow roses successfully, we, as children's caregivers, must be dedicated to obtaining the knowledge of experts in child development. Emotional development involves many learned behaviors. Human beings grow from infancy to toddlers; toddlers grow to school age. How healthily they develop depends upon how knowledgeable (or deficient) their caregivers (parents, guardians, child-care providers, teachers) are. Information was shared and demonstrated significance because children develop self-regulation and other coping skills by modeling the adults with whom they interact. For this reason, positive relationships are vital.

Studies in the three areas of child development also revealed that children develop cognitively as they develop socially and emotionally and that their social and emotional needs play a role in the learning (cognitive) process. We delved briefly into brain research and other studies on how the brain develops from infancy to school age. Information about brain research indicates that children are ready to learn specific cognitive skills at different ages and levels of mental development. Therefore, children's caregivers must provide precise, age-appropriate activities that accommodate the level children are mentally ready to learn.

Parents are brought into the picture as their perspectives on their children's educational process are investigated. Interviews with parents set the groundwork for conversations around this issue. The intention was not to answer any question but to stimulate awareness of the support parents may need to nurture and connect to their children's educational experiences. Parents' perspectives showed that effective communication was fundamental to nurturing the connection. To communicate effectively, dialogue cannot be blamed; on the contrary, it should be open, trusting, and welcoming.

Readers are reminded that children are little human beings with minds, bodies, and spirits. Children need more than food for their bodies; their minds also need nourishment that encourages the body to develop healthily. Nourishment in the form of unconditional love produces a child with a loving, secure spirit. In the same way that flowers flourish when adequately nurtured, studies show that nurturing school and home environments positively affect children.

It explained why and how to create nurturing environments for young children and provided suggestions for children's caregivers that encouraged communication, collaboration, and unconditional love. Because children get cues from adults in their lives, caregivers must also be mindful of their relationships and interactions with each other. In addition, it is crucial to recognize the personal sacrifices one must be willing to make when caring for children. Every adult who has accepted this vital responsibility must hold himself or herself accountable for the emotional, social, and cognitive health of the children in his or her care. I desire Nurture to provide insight into this critical undertaking precisely and beneficially.

About the Author

With over **25** years of dedicated service, Mattie Lee Jones, PhD, has passionately supported young children's social, emotional, and cognitive development and well-being. Her roles as a teacher, school principal, and higher education administrator have allowed her to impact the lives of numerous children, adults, caregivers, guardians, and teachers, instilling confidence in her extensive experience and expertise.

As many call her, Dr. Mattie was a longtime member of The National Association for the Education of Young Children (NAEYC) and the Indiana Association for the Education of Young Children (IAEYC), where she served as Vice President. She also received the IAEYC Educator Award.

Dr. Mattie received training and certification in Trauma-Informed Care and Adverse Childhood Experiences (ACES). In addition, she was instrumental in creating a trauma-informed Curriculum as the Dean of the School of Education at an Indiana University.

Dr. Mattie's profound experience with children and their parents has fueled her to write her first book, "Missing Link?" which delves into parents' perspectives on their children's education. Her unwavering passion for research, evident in her second book, "What Did Your Parents Do To You," a collection of true stories that unveil childhood events and relationships with parents and guardians that may have influenced their life journeys and parenting styles, is truly inspiring.

Dr. Mattie's books are not just theoretical but also practical. She has spent many years using her experience and expertise to train and support childcare workers and childcare owners. Upon a request by childcare owners, she penned the book "Disciplining Someone Else's Children" (A Guide for Classroom & School Management). This book is a practical guide based on her firsthand experiences in over 15 schools in Indiana and childcare facilities. It reflects her findings and serves as a guide to providing what was needed in the training she conducted with the childcare facility staff and teachers.

In the book "Nurture," Dr. Mattie demonstrates how children's social, emotional, and cognitive development are connected and how children will thrive now and into adulthood by creating nurturing environments. The second edition of the book Nurture II allowed her to research and look deeply into nurturing traumatized children. It reveals the urgency for the nurturing approach to trauma for all children and adults, emphasizing the importance of her work.

Reference List

Part One

- C:\Users\Jones\Downloads\qrcode_www.tedmed.com.png
- https://www.chcs.org/welcome-upswing-state-federal-support-trauma-informed-practice-policies
- https://www.tedmed.com/talks/show?id=293066
- https://www.nctsn.org/what-is-child-trauma/about-child-trauma
- https://www.nctsn.org/treatments-and-practices/core-curriculum-childhood-trauma
- http://www.acf.hhs.gov>toxicstress
- http://www.turnto23.com
- Traumaticinformedcare.chc.org
- https://parenting.ra6.org/nurturing-enviroment.htm
- youth.gov/feature-article/samhsas-concept-trauma-and-guidance-trauma-informed-approach.org
- Book "Nurture" 2016, iUniverse rev. date: 11/23/2016, by Dr. Mattie Lee Jones
- https://www.ncbi.nim.nih.gov/pm/articles/PMC3774302/

Part Two

- American Academy of Pediatrics, https://www.aap.org, accessed 2016

- America's Children in Brief: Key National Indicators of Well-Being, www.Childstats. gov/americaschildren, 2015

- Bell, M. & Wolfe, C. (2004). Emotion and Cognition: An Intricately Bound

- Developmental Process in Child Development 75 (2): 36670 Feb. 2004.

- Birch, S., & Ladd, G. Interpersonal Relationship in the School Environment & Children's Early School Adjustment: The Role of Teachers & Peers, (1996).

- Campbell, F. A., Early Learning Later Success: The Abecedarian Study, http://fpg. unc.edu/resouce/early-learning-later-success-abecedarian-study Process Child Development, (2000). Vol. 75 No. 2, 366–70.

- Child Action: The Importance of Play, www.childaction.org/families/publications/ docs/guidance/handout13-the importance of play.pdf, accessed 2016

- Cherry, Kendra "What is Art Therapy," www.verywell.com-2795755 (2016): Essentials for Childhood Framework: Steps to Create Safe, Stable, Nurturing Relationship and Environment for Children, The National Center

- for Injury Prevention & Control www.cdcgov/violenceprevention/ pdf/essentials for childhood framework.pdf, August 2014 (p.7)

- Dusenbury, Linda PhD, "Creating a Safe Classroom Environment" Education World article, educationworld.com/a_curry/creating-safe-classroom environment- climates.shtml accessed 2016

- Facts for Life, "Child Development & Early Learning Facts", 4th edition, www. factsforlifeglobal.org/03/1.html accessed 2016

- Gable, Sara "Nature, Nurture and Early Brain Development" article 30, May 3, 2008, www.classbrain.com

- Galinsky, Ellen "Mind in the Making, Seven Essential Life Skills Every Child Needs," 1st edition, pp 321–322. (2010)

- Kushnir, Tamar, "Learning about How Children Learn," Cornell University, www. human.cornell.edu/nd/outreach/upload/ learning-about-how-children-learn- Kushnir, (2009).

- Laughlin, Lynda "Who's Minding the Kids?" www.census.gov/ prod/2013pubs/ page70-135, (April 2013)

- Mental Health America, www.metalhealthamerica.net, (2016) The National Association for the Education of Young Children, www.Naeyc.org/ DAP, Accessed 2016

- Perry, Bruce MD, PhD "How Children Learn Language" Early Childhood Today, scholastic.com/teachers/article/how-young-children-learn-language (2016)

- Sagan, C., A. Druyan "Literacy the Path to a More Prosperous Less Dangerous America" Parade magazine, March 6, 1994.

- Jones (Solomon), Mattie Lee, "Disciplining Someone Else's Children, "iUniverse (2015).

- Jones (Solomon), Mattie Lee, "What Did Your Parents Do to You," (iUniverse, 2014).

- Jones (Solomon), Mattie Lee, Missing Link? iUniverse. (2011).

- Winfrey, Oprah "What I Know for Sure," Flatiron Books (September 2014).

- The American Rose Society (ARS), www.rose.org, accessed 2016

- The National Center for Injury Prevention (CDC) www.cdc.gov/violenceprevention. Accessed 2016

- The National Association for the Education of Young Children (NAEYC), www.naeyc.org accessed 2016

- The Human Memory www.human-memory.net/brain neurons.html.(2010),

Printed in the United States
by Baker & Taylor Publisher Services